DISABILITY: FUTURE MARKET DEMAND AND COSTS OF LONG-TERM SERVICES AND SUPPORTS

DISABILITY: FUTURE MARKET DEMAND AND COSTS OF LONG-TERM SERVICES AND SUPPORTS

MICHAEL MORRIS
AND
JOHNETTE HARTNETT

Nova Science Publishers, Inc.
New York

Copyright © 2009 by Nova Science Publishers, Inc.

Library of Congress Cataloging-in-Publication Data

Morris, Michael, 1977-
  Disability : future market demand and costs of long-term services and supports / Michael Morris and Johnette Harnett (authors).
    p. ; cm.
  ISBN 978-1-60692-251-4 (softcover)
  1. People with disabilities--Long-term care--Economic aspects--United States. 2. People with disabilities--Long-term care--United States--Costs. 3. People with disabilities--Long-term care--Government policy--United States. I. Hartnett, Johnette. II. Title.
  [DNLM: 1. Disabled Persons--rehabilitation--United States. 2. Rehabilitation--economics--United States. 3. Health Services Needs and Demand--trends--United States. 4. Long-Term Care--economics--United States. WB 320 M877d 2009]
  RA644.6.M67 2009
  362.4068--dc22
                              2008038238

Published by Nova Science Publishers, Inc. New York

CONTENTS

Part I

INTRODUCING RESEARCH PURPOSE
AND THE RICH PICTURE STORY LINE

Purpose

The purpose of this book is to explore and understand the future market demand and costs of long-term services and supports (LTSS) for individuals with disabilities through a review and analysis of the literature and in-depth case studies of six individuals to better understand the current experience with and future need for affordable LTSS nationwide for Americans with disabilities.

Rich Picture Story Line [337]

The setting for this book is the LTSS ship heading toward the iceberg in the waters of reform. The iceberg represents barriers to reform; the state of the economy; state and federal deficits; rising health care costs; workforce shortages; increasing numbers of uninsured; low national savings; and increased longevity of all Americans. The setting in part II is an overview of the storm clouds: multidimensional financial and attitudinal challenges that compete for the attention of even the most skilled navigators. In part III, the consumer-directors chart their way through the demographic challenges and trends of the current and future LTSS system. The setting in part IV is the LTSS ship with its consumer-directors talking with other Medicaid beneficiaries about the rising costs. The waves are taking their toll, and it becomes evident that some passengers must be lowered onto lifeboats and given passage to safer waters. In part V, the ship will come face to face with the financial barriers to reform and lower its lifeboats yet again before hitting the iceberg. In part VI, six consumer-directors will introduce themselves and provide information about their journey and what they think their lives will look like in 2030. In part VII, the consumer-directors will summarize their findings and prepare for their final voyage into the waters of reform.

Research Questions

The Government Accountability Office (GAO) states clearly in its "21st Century Challenges: Reexamining the Federal Base of Government" that current fiscal policies in place today are economically unsustainable over the long term without unprecedented changes in tax and/or spending policies. [338] The report identifies emerging forces that are carving out a new position for the United States in the world today. Several of these forces—long-term fiscal imbalance, increasing global interdependence, changing economy, demographic shifts, science and technology advances, and quality-of-life trends—will directly impact the current and future viability of LTSS for Americans with disabilities. In addition, the report poses a set of 21st century questions intended to guide Congress in addressing current fiscal demands as well as future fiscal challenges in fine-tuning current and future public policy that covers discretionary spending, mandatory spending (including entitlements), and tax policies. [339]

> Defining differences between needs, wants, affordability, and sustainability is fundamental to rethinking the design of our current health care system.
>
> **GAO-05-325SP**

This book will probe answers to the following questions:

- Who needs LTSS?
- How is the population projected to change over the next 25 years?
- What are the pathways for eligibility for LTSS and have they changed?
- Who is meeting the LTSS demands and financing them?
- What do we know about LTSS costs today and in the future?

Part II

FORECASTING THE STORM

Overview of the Problem

The United States is a nation at risk at it enters the 21st century with unsustainable social and fiscal policy to support its aging and disability population. Despite two centuries of economic progress, it is still without a sustainable internal infrastructure for the delivery of affordable health care and LTSS for all Americans. [340, 341, 342] Because of the intersection of many demographic changes over the next century—such as increased longevity; low fertility rates; changing patterns of marriage, divorce, and participation in the labor force and immigration; lower national savings; rising state deficits and health care costs—there is great concern about the future of LTSS for Americans with disabilities. [343, 344, 345]

The director of the Congressional Budget Office (CBO), in testimony on Social Security reform before the Committee on the Budget, U.S. House of Representatives, on February 9, 2005, testified that "a major achievement of reform is to resolve uncertainty about the future and that uncertainty is an economic cost in its most fundamental form . . . and the sooner the uncertainty is resolved the better served future beneficiaries will be." [346] The director stated that the key uncertainty stems from a central policy question: To what extent should Social Security programs in the 21st century resemble the program in the 20th century? The Consortium for Citizens with Disabilities responded that Congress should request a beneficiary impact statement for every major component of any serious proposal and that, when evaluating any program that affects millions of individuals of all ages, it is essential for policymakers to look beyond the budgetary change to understand the actual impact on people's daily lives. [347]

There are 38 million Americans under age 65 reporting some level of disability [348] and, of this group, 25 million (11 percent of the nonelderly population) have a specific chronic disability. [349] Fifty-three percent have private insurance, 20 percent are covered under Medicaid, 15 percent are uninsured, and 12 percent have Medicare and other types of insurance. [350] There are 8.1 million Americans with disabilities on Medicaid and another 6 million on Medicare who are under age 65. [351] The Medicaid beneficiaries with disabilities are substantially more impaired than other individuals with disabilities. About 50 percent have a physical impairment, one-fourth have some limitation in performing activities of daily living (ADLs), and 40 percent have severe mental symptoms or disorders. [352]

Most of the research on aging defines a person as needing LTSS if he or she requires another person's help with one or more ADLs or instrumental activities of daily living (IADLs). Using this definition, there are 9.5 million people with LTSS needs, and 36 percent (3.56 million) are nonelderly, including residents of nursing home and intermediate care facilities for the mentally retarded (ICF/MRs). [353]

The comptroller general of the GAO has called for a "fundamental reexamination" of America's spending and tax priorities because of the mounting long-term fiscal challenges primarily caused by known demographic trends and growing health care costs. [354] A national forum of leading experts convened to explore the gap in public understanding of the nature and magnitude of the long-term fiscal challenge and to examine strategies for marketing the problem to the public to begin the dialogue about solutions. The problem was described as "too big to be solved by economic growth, or making modest changes to existing spending and tax policy." [355] The seriousness of the problem is reflected in the growing imbalance between discretionary and mandatory spending. In 1964, two-thirds (67 percent) of total federal spending was discretionary; in FY 2004, this share had shrunk to about 39 percent. [356]

Key barriers identified at the national forum were similar to the barriers identified in chapter 1 of this report: gaining public and political will; lack of consensus among leaders on the nature, extent, and timing of the nation's fiscal problem; lack of possible solutions; and lack of public understanding of the problem. [357] This phenomenon is perplexing: Despite years of national symposiums, thousands of published research studies, and millions of dollars spent on the economics of America's troubled social and fiscal policy, we are still without reform. [358]

Testimony on the crisis in long-term care (LTC) spending was heard on April 19, 2005, before the Subcommittee on Health of the House Committee on Ways and Means, U.S. House of Representatives. Noticeably absent was research about the service and support needs and challenges of people with disabilities who are under the age of 65. Congress and the American public still think only of aging when they discuss issues of LTSS. Even the research is scarce on the prevalence and demographics of people using LTSS under age 65. As the current debate heats up, it will be imperative that disability research is developed that provides comprehensive data on what it costs to live with a lifelong disability.

The current system of LTSS is based on policy and purpose written 40 years ago for low-income Americans on public assistance, children, the elderly, and people with disabilities. Although Medicaid and Medicare have made many improvements over the past four decades, their fundamental purposes were not designed to meet the needs of the current aging and disability demographics. Today, less than 20 percent of people on Medicaid are on welfare; 30 percent of the population includes the elderly and people with disabilities, and the other 70 percent includes mostly children and families who need health insurance. [359] Despite legislation that allows states to shift services and supports from the nursing home to the community, Medicaid continues to spend 64.3 percent ($73.1 billion) for care in nursing facilities and ICF/MRs, mainly for people with disabilities. [360] Medicaid spending has gone from 8 percent of state budgets in 1985 to 22 percent in 2003. [361] Seven million people with disabilities receive both Medicaid and Medicare (dual eligible) and account for 42 percent of all state Medicaid spending. [362]

Although Americans make more money than the rest of the world, they spend more. [363] Many people with disabilities and seniors who are not eligible for public benefits are not financially prepared to pay for the costs of LTSS (only 7% have annual incomes of $50,000 or more). [364, 365]A private room in a nursing home in 2003 was $66,000 on average and a home health aide averaged $18 per hour. People with disabilities under age 65 are poorer and have less work history than today's retired seniors (35% have incomes hovering around the federal poverty level). Individuals with disabilities on Supplemental Security Income (SSI) who are working (more than 323,000) are challenged by disincentives in the policy that discourage earnings and prevent the development of assets that could provide resources to pay a fair share of the costs for LTSS. [366]

Few Americans with lifelong impairments purchase LTC insurance because of the cost and the reluctance of the insurance industry to underwrite high-risk populations. [367, 368] Yet, a few major investment houses are marketing financial planning products for special needs populations, which appeal to parents challenged with providing for the long-term future of a child with a lifelong disability. Ten percent of Americans have purchased LTC insurance, but for people with disabilities, many of the standard policies cater more to medical rehabilitation and less to the nonspecific needs of those who have a chronic illness or long-term impairment. Under the current system, it is unclear how families and communities plan to support a child born today with a lifelong disability that will require extraordinary costs.

The trend to drop employer-based health care is growing as annual health care premiums continue to rise. [369] The Institute of Medicine estimates that 18,000 lives are lost each year because of gaps in insurance coverage at an economic cost between $65 billion and $139 billion annually from premature death, preventable disability, early retirement, and reduced economic output. [370]

The shrinking workforce, both paid and unpaid, providing the majority of LTSS is unstable, underpaid, and untrained. [371] The family unit that provides the majority of unpaid care today (women in their 50s) will change in the future. [372] More women are opting out of motherhood and remaining single or divorced. [373]

America must construct a new system for individuals who need LTSS to go to school, to work, or to be retired at home. Most important, it needs a system that will promote independence and self-sufficiency in an affordable and dignified way.

Part III

TRACKING THE STORM

Demographic Trends in Long-Term Services and Supports

Defining Long-Term Services and Supports

The 21st century LTSS policy is guided by a strong federal and state commitment toward home- and community-based services (HCBS) and is an important milestone for people with disabilities. The shifting of costs from institutional spending to community-based service spending is providing the infrastructure and capacity for people with disabilities to work, go to school, and live independently. The evolution of the current system of LTSS requires a definition that identifies the scope and depth of services needed that is inclusive of people with disabilities under the age of 65. [374]

The NCD supports a broad definition of LTSS that reflects the essential needs for maintaining a quality of life with maximum dignity and independence. Housing, transportation, nutrition, technology, personal assistance, and other social supports are included in the NCD definition of LTSS. [375]

The AARP definition of long-terms services and supports provides a good overview of the breadth and depth of what a long-term services and support policy means today:

> LTSS refers to a wide range of in-home, community-based, and institutional services and programs that are designed to help individuals of all ages with physical or mental impairments who have lost or never acquired the ability to function independently. LTSS include assistance with performing self-care

activities and household tasks, habilitation and rehabilitation, adult day services, case management, social services, assistive technology, job modification, and some medical care. LTSS are provided in a variety of settings, including at home, in assisted living and other supportive housing settings, and in nursing homes. [376]

The AARP Policy Book explains that people with disabilities prefer to use the phrase "long-term services and supports" rather than "long-term care" because of possible implications concerning dependence or paternalism. The movement to provide services and supports in the community rather than in an institution is the result largely of the work of disability advocates who have worked for decades to control the direction of their services and supports outside the traditional facility or institution. Federal and state legislation and the Supreme Court have responded with a flurry of demonstration projects and decisions that have favored noninstitutional living. However, federal and state Medicaid spending for LTSS continues to favor institutional care (nursing facilities and ICF/MRs), with the balance spent on HCBS. [377]

The Congressional Research Service (CRS) found that different disability groups have focused on different aspects of consumer-directed LTSS to fit their individual needs, including the use of individual budgets and other self-empowering strategies for managing and directing their own services and supports. [378] The CRS reported that

Individuals with physical disabilities and who are aging have generally focused on personal care services. For individuals with developmental disabilities, consumer direction has been referred to as "self-determination" and has often included other long-term care services in addition to personal care services, such as respite and adult day care. For individuals with serious and persistent mental illness, opportunities for consumers to direct their own services have not been as prevalent, although there is a growing interest in consumer empowerment, peer-support services, and peer participation in treatment. [379]

No research found estimated overall costs for an individual with a lifelong impairment based on the definitions used here for LTSS. The productivity losses, societal costs, direct medical and nonmedical utilization rates, housing, and living expenses for a person living with a lifelong disability are important statistical data that when aggregated would help build a true economic picture for policy and budget discussion. There are studies that have looked at prevalence and mortality rates of particular categories of disability but have not included other relevant variables about what it takes for a family to raise a child with a severe chronic lifelong disability. [380]

The importance of introducing a new definition for LTSS is that it will describe to policymakers and budget directors the unique issues and economic profile of living with a disability under the age of 65. The current focus on LTC for people over 65 was underscored in an April 2004 paper from the CBO on "Financing Long-Term Care for the Elderly." One page was dedicated to "nonelderly people." The study found that, in general, people younger than 65 use LTC services for different reasons than people over 65 years of age, referring to mental illness, mental retardation, and neurological conditions. [381] The CBO paper does report that Medicaid is the largest funder for LTC for impaired people under the age of 65 and that, since 1992, the program has grown 4.8 percent annually. The CBO report is directed to Congress and provides little information about the LTSS needs of people with disabilities under the age of 65, other than that they are mostly Medicaid dependent. It is clear that Congress would need more information about the 14 million Americans under age 65 on Medicaid and Medicare to better understand the demographics, costs, and service needs of those receiving LTSS through public programs who are working, going to school, living at home, or retired. New LTSS policy must include not only the aging cohort of Americans with disabilities but also the under-65 cohort.

When actuaries prepare assumptions about the future, they look at a number of factors. The actual future income and expenditures for a new system of LTSS will depend on many factors, including the size and characteristics of the population receiving benefits, the size and level of benefit amounts, and the number of workers and their earnings. None of the proposals for reforming the current LTSS system provided assumptions about future costs (see chapter 3) that included the full array of factors, such as the following: birthrates, death rates, immigration, marriage and divorce rates, retirement-age patterns, disability incidence and termination rates, production gains, wage increases, medical and nonmedical costs, inflation, and many other demographic, economic, and program-specific factors. [382]

Even demographic data about the nonelderly users of LTSS who are living in institutions (including group homes) is not readily available, because the various surveys used to collect this data do not encompass all institutional settings. [383] The Disability Supplement to the National Health Interview Survey (NHIS-D) is a household survey of nonelderly community dwellers and does not include group homes that in 2004 represented about 7 percent of the population with mental retardation and developmental disabilities (MR/DD). The National Long-Term Care Survey (NLTCS) draws from Medicare enrollment files and community and institutional residents, and the researchers found that "no such population-based survey exists for the non-elderly using long-term services and supports and no combination of existing surveys can be said with confidence to provide a similarly comprehensive view of the non-elderly." [384] One survey did collect data in 1987—the National Medical Expenditure Survey, Institutional Population Component—and, at the time, did include nursing homes, ICF/MRs, and licensed personal care homes for residents of all ages. [385] However, its successor survey in 1996—the Medicaid Expenditure Panel Survey (MEPS)—restricted data collection to nursing homes only. The authors estimated that about 416,000, or 0.4 million people (MR/DD and mentally ill in state mental institutions, residential facilities, government general hospitals, private hospitals, and VA medical centers), are left out of national surveys of nonelderly recipients of LTSS. This population is not always reflected in the national figures used to represent the number of people under 65 years of age needing services and supports.

Table 2.1 combines two national survey data sets to compare community-based service use and nursing home use for individuals under 65 years of age with nonusers of community service. Females are more likely to receive community-based services and be in nursing homes than males in the general public; 4.8 percent of community-based service users are widowed, compared with 10.3 percent of nursing home residents and 1.8 percent of nonusers; individuals receiving both community-based services and nursing home services were 50 percent more likely to have an education of less than 12 years; and community-based users had twice the poverty rate of nonusers. [386] There was no single data set to provide national estimates for elderly and nonelderly LTC users in both community and institutional settings. [387]

Table 2.1. Demographics of Long-Term Service and Supports, Community-Based Users and Nonusers [388]

Characteristics	Nonusers of Community Services	Community-Based Services Use <65	Nursing Home Residents <65
Population (Thousands)	155,200 (97.8%)	3,364 (2.1%)	138 (0.1%)
Mean Age (Years)	38	45	51
Gender Female Male	50.8 49.2	57.6 42.4	51.0 49.0
Race White Black Other	83.2 12.0 04.9	77.0 19.0 04.0	76.1 19.2 04.7

Table 2.1. Continued

Characteristics	Nonusers of Community Services	Community-Based Services Use <65	Nursing Home Residents <65
Population (Thousands)	155,200 (97.8%)	3,364 (2.1%)	138 (0.1%)
Mean Age (Years)	38	45	51
Marital Status			
Married	65.9	57.3	16.4
Widowed	01.8	04.8	10.3
Never Married	22.0	29.2	46.3
Separated/Divorced	10.2	18.4	27.0
Education			
Less Than 12 Years	15.3	34.3	42.0
12 Years	37.1	39.4	23.8
Greater Than 12 Years	46.9	23.5	16.9
Missing	0.70	02.7	16.4
Poverty	10.2	26.0	N/A
Level of IADL/ADL Disability			
IADL Only	N/A	55.9	07.7
1-2 Adls	N/A	26.7	14.5
3-6 ADLS	N/A	17.4	75.5
Functional Limitations			
Lower Body Only	05.1	33.3	N/A
Upper Body Only	00.8	1.6	N/A
Upper And Lower Body	01.5	38.1	N/A
Neither	92.2	26.2	N/A
Use of Mobility Equipment	00.8	25.0	13.0
Use of Wheelchair	00.1	12.7	65.2
Difficulty Seeing	01.6	17.4	30.2
Difficulty Hearing	03.5	11.3	12.8
Difficulty Communication	00.3	11.6	16.6
Difficulty Understanding	00.4	09.8	12.0
Mental Retardation	00.1	11.6	N/A

N/A = not available.

People Who Use Long-Term Services and Supports

The development of public policy for LTSS requires finding a common ground for defining eligibility. The review of the literature found definitions for disability that identify function (ADLs, IADLs), chronic illness, children with chronic illness, census data on perceived disability, and work disability. The accepted definitions of eligibility are the two major ones, provided by Medicaid and SSI, which are used most often in the literature and are the gateway to services and supports for millions of Americans with disabilities.

Seventy-eight percent (5.6 million) of people with disabilities in FY 2000 enrolled in Medicaid through SSI; the remaining 22 percent (8.1 million) were categorized as "other" (some on Medicare). It is estimated that about 25 million Americans under the age of 65 with chronic disabilities need some help with ADLs [389] but often do not meet the criteria of total disability required by Social Security until their conditions are in the advanced stage. [390] Examples include people with HIV and multiple sclerosis. The CRS data estimates that 3.4 million people with disabilities under age 65 receive an array of LTSS (mostly in their homes and unpaid), but this varies depending on each state's fiscal capacity or changing economic condition.

Emerging Demographics of Long-Term Service and Support Use

Trends for chronic disease and disabilities are showing increases. The prevalence of chronic disease and deaths caused by noncommunicable disease in the United States between 1990 and 2020 will increase from 28.1 million to 49.7 million, an increase of 77 percent. Overall heart disease, in terms of both death and disability, will be greater than any other illness. Cancer will rank second. By the year 2010, mental illness, namely unipolar major depression, will have a greater impact on death and disability than cancer. [391] Medicaid has become the principal public payer of mental health services at 36 percent, with Medicare spending 22 percent, and state and local governments spending 35 percent with another 7 percent coming from the Federal Government, totaling $48 billion. [392] The most common chronic disability conditions relate to mental health, mental retardation, cognitive impairment, and learning disability.

The impacts of these trends and further analyses have varied predictions for prevalence and future health care costs. However, the challenge inherent in consolidating the medical and nonmedical needs for LTSS into population characteristics with cost estimates differs based on criteria and the definition of disability used. The following definitions and estimates of disability prevalence are good examples of how complex and confusing this can be.

Use of ADLs and IADLs in Measuring Functional Ability

The definitions used in describing the ability of individuals to function independently in the community are ADLs and IADLs. ADLs include a person's ability to perform the following functions: bathing, dressing, eating, toileting, getting in or out of bed or a chair, and getting around inside the home. IADLs include preparing meals, going outside the home, managing money, using the telephone, taking prescription medications, and doing housework. [393] For people with intellectual impairments, the ADL and IADL criteria do not always accurately represent their functioning capacity. Further research is being done on expanding criteria to better serve people with intellectual impairments. The estimate of community-based LTSS, among the nonelderly is 2.1 percent (over 3.4 million) receiving assistance with ADL or IADL tasks.

The likelihood of needing help with ADLs rises with age. It is estimated that, by age 65, 10 to 20 percent of individuals will require assistance with at least one or more ADL and that, by age 85, 50 percent will require assistance. [394] Demographers predict a dramatic impact on the prevalence of disability and use of LTSS in the coming decades. People who need help with at least two ADLs will increase from 1.8 million (1996–2000) to 3.8 million (2045–-2049). The number of nursing home residents and residents in alternative living facilities over age 65 will increase from 2 million in 2000 to 2.6 million in 2020 and 4.5 million in 2050. The number of home-based services users will increase from 5.4 million in 2000 to 7.2 million in 2020 to 10.5 million in 2050. [395]

The research concludes that disability has declined in the over-65 population for those who reported needing help with IADLs. The decline represented a 3.9 percentage point decline in elderly people receiving help from someone with ADLs and IADLs and a 1.4 percentage point increase in elderly people who managed ADLs in the community with assistive devices only. [396] The study also found a 3.7 percentage point drop in help with money management between 1984 and 1989, when Social Security direct deposit became the norm, raising the question of whether IADL declines reflect improvements in health or improvements in the physical environment. Researchers suggest that the overall decline may be driven by environmental and not health-related changes. Increases in technology and greater availability of services and durable medical equipment, including assistive technology, are thought to have contributed to the decline. The mean number of IADLs for which people with disabilities received assistance declined over the 15-year study, but the mean number of ADLs for which assistance was received increased for people with disabilities living in institutions and in the community. If the IADL rate continues to decline, researchers will study the relationship among savings in Medicare, Medicaid, and LTSS. [397]

Table 2.2. Disability Definitions

Disability Categories	Disability Definitions	Demographics
Functional [398]	Limits in or inability to perform a variety of physical activity, serious sensory impairment (e.g., unable to read a newspaper, even with glasses), serious symptoms of mental illness, long-term care needs, use of an assistive device (e.g., wheelchair), developmental delay in a child that is identified by a physician, and inability to perform age-appropriate functions.	47.6 million Americans 6.1 million children 25.7 million working-age adults 15.8 million elderly
Work [399]	Limitations or the inability to work as a result of a physical, mental, or emotional health condition.	16.9 million working-age adults (18-64 years of age)
Perceived [400]	Individuals who reported that they considered themselves to have a disability or were considered by others to have a disability.	19 million Americans 2 million children 11.1 adults (18-63 years of age) 6 million elderly
Public Program Recipients Under Age 65 [401]	Includes people covered by government funding programs, Special Education or Early Intervention Services, and/or disability pensions.	13.8 million individuals 4.7 million children 9.1 million adults age 18-64 65 and older not included in this definition

Definitions of disability in the literature vary from ICD-9 Codes to subjective criteria, such as a child's ability to play. The scope of the population with disabilities was not consistent; for example, parameters such as age range, setting of services, and service types used to segment and measure the population. In addition to the use of ADLs and IADLs, four additional definitions are listed in table 2.2.

A study from the Research Institute and Training Center on Community Living at the University of Minnesota examined the service use by and needs of adults with functional limitations (FLs) or intellectual disabilities/developmental disabilities (ID/DD) between the ages of 18–35 and 35–64. The researchers found that people with ID/DD have substantially more limitations in ADLs, learning, communication, self-direction, and economic self-sufficiency compared with people with FLs only. Women with ID/DD 35 years and older were more likely to have economic problems than women under age 35 with FLs only. Gender differences were found in the two populations—more males were found in both age categories with ID/DD and more females were found in the FL category age 35 and older. This study has important policy implications because it suggests that, within different categories of disability, there are different service needs that get overlooked, and that a more careful study of the gender and age differences between groups may be needed.

Another challenge for individuals with disabilities under the age of 65 with personal assistance needs is receiving the necessary hours of support. A recent study estimated the shortfall in hours of help and adverse consequences and found that individuals who needed help with two or more of the five basic ADLs had a shortfall of 16.6 hours of help per week compared with those whose needs are met. [402] Those with unmet needs were more likely to be nonwhite, to be female, and to live alone. The shortfall in hours as a percentage of needed hours is twice as great for people who live alone. Both groups in the study found those who live with someone and those who live alone experienced adverse consequences in 29 out of the 34 measures tested, including weight loss, dehydration, falls, burns, and dissatisfaction with the help received. People who live alone and have unmet needs are 10 times as likely to go hungry, 20 times more likely to miss a meal, and 5 times as likely to lose weight. [403]

Personal assistance services (PAS) are provided to about 13.2 million noninstitutionalized adults, representing an average of 31.4 hours of PAS each week. [404] Of these, 3.2 million people received an average of 17.6 hours of paid help, and 11.7 million received an average of 30.7 hours of unpaid help. This study found that older people are likely to receive paid PAS and that working-age people rely more on unpaid PAS.

The policy implications of these studies suggest that future LTSS policy should consider the number of working individuals under age 65, their specific needs for PAS, and the impact that adequate and consistent PAS might have on future earnings and long-term employment for working-age individuals with disabilities.

Children and the Need for Long-Term Services and Supports

A report by the U.S. Department of Health and Human Services (HHS), "Children with Severe Chronic Conditions on Medicaid," used 360 disease-specific codes (ICD-9 Codes) to define children with physical and mental health disabilities. [405] In addition to the diagnosis codes, the criteria for disability included hospital utilization criteria. Physical disability utilization criteria included the following:

- 3 or more hospital admissions;
- 20 or more days of inpatient hospital care;
- total outpatient payment of $5,000 or more; and
- total payment of $20,000 or more.

Mental health disability criteria included the following:

- 30 days or more of inpatient hospital care with any of the primary psychiatric diagnoses; and
- outpatient payments of $5,000 or more for any of the primary psychiatric diagnoses. [406]

A 1995 summary by the Assistant Secretary for Planning and Evaluation (ASPE) identified 4,536,300 American children with disabilities. This report defined disability as difficulty with certain functions or abilities (e.g., playing) because of a physical or mental health impairment. [407] This summary also stated that determining the prevalence of disability was difficult due to varied definitions; however, it reported that 4,536,300 children in the United States had a disability and that 98 percent lived in the community and 2 percent (91,800) lived in institutions; 1,200 children lived in nursing homes; and 1,100 lived in homes for individuals with physical disabilities. Another 29,500 children were in facilities for the mentally ill, and 60,000 were in MR/DD facilities. [408] The report did note that there are 148,000 children in correctional facilities, on whom data on disability was not available.

Of the 51 American million children ages 5 through 17 in 1994, less than 1 percent were likely to need LTSS; 1.3 percent had problems with mobility; 5.5 percent with communication; 10.6 percent with learning; 12.3 percent needed help with one or more ADLs; and 0.9 percent were likely to need LTSS for self-care. Fifty-nine percent of people with MR/DD are under the age of 17; 38 percent are between 17 and 64 years of age; and 3 percent are over the age of 65. [409]

The leading causes of disability in children reported in the 1995 ASPE summary were learning disabilities (1,372,200), speech disorders (1,096,000), MR/DD (720,500), mental illness (462,800), and respiratory conditions such as asthma (362,200). [410]

People Over Age 65

In 1999, people 65 years or older numbered 34.5 million. This represents 12.7 percent of the U.S. population, about one in every eight Americans. The number of older Americans has increased 3.3 million (10.6) percent since 1990, compared with an increase of 9.1 percent for the under-65 population. [411]

Since 1900, the percentage of Americans over 65 has tripled, and the number has increased 11 times, from 3.1 million to 34.5 million. [412] A child born in 1998 could expect to live 76.7 years, about 29 years longer than a child born in 1900. The major part of this increase is due to reduced death rates for children and young adults. Two million people turned 65 in 1999 (5,422 per day). In the same year, 1.8 million people 65 years of age or older died, resulting in a net increase of 200,000 (558) per day. [413] Life expectancy in the United States rose dramatically in the 20th century from about 47 years in 1900 to about 73 years for males and 79 years for females in 1999. This increase is mainly due to improvements in environmental factors, such as sanitation, and the discovery of antibiotics. [414]

By 2030, there will be about 70 million Americans over the age of 65. People over 65 represented 13 percent of the population in 1999; this percentage will grow to 20 percent by 2030. Minority populations are projected to represent 25.4 percent of the elderly population in 2030, up from 16.1 percent in 1999. [415]

In 1998, the majority (67%) of the elderly was noninstitutionalized and lived in a family setting. Approximately 10.8 million (80%) of older men and 10.7 million (58%) of older women lived in families. The proportion living with a family decreased with age. Forty-five percent of those over 85 years lived in a family setting. About 13 percent of older people (7% men, 17% women) were not living with a spouse but were living with children, siblings, or other relatives.

About 3 percent of men and 2 percent of women (718,000) of the older population lived with nonrelatives. [416] A small number (1.47 million, 4.3%) of the over-65 population lived in nursing homes in 1997, and the percentage increased dramatically with age, ranging from 1.1 percent for people 65–74 years to 4.5 percent for people 75–84 years and 19 percent for people over the age of 85. [417]

In 1999, 16.1 percent of people over age 65 were minorities: 8.1 percent were African American, 2.3 percent were Asian, and less than 1 percent were American Indian or Native Alaskan. Hispanic origins represented 5.3 percent of the older population. [418]

In 1999, about half (52%) of people over age 65 lived in nine states: California had over 3.6 million; Florida, 2.7 million; New York, 2.4 million; Texas, 2 million; and Pennsylvania, 1.9 million. Ohio, Illinois, Michigan, and New Jersey each had over 1 million. [419]

In 1999, people over 65 constituted 14 percent or more of the total population in 10 states: Florida, 18.1 percent; Pennsylvania, 15.8 percent; Rhode Island, 15.6 percent; West Virginia, 15.1 percent; Iowa, 14.9 percent; North Dakota, 14.6 percent; South Dakota, 14.4 percent; Connecticut, 14.3 percent; Arkansas, 14.2 percent; and Maine, 14 percent. In 11 states, the over-65 population increased by 17 percent or more between 1990 and 1999: Nevada, 61 percent; Alaska, 55 percent; Arizona, 31 percent; Hawaii, 30 percent; Colorado, Utah, and New Mexico, 23 percent; Delaware, 21 percent; South Carolina and North Carolina, 19 percent; and Texas, 17 percent. [420]

Table 2.3. Population Projections Five-Year Age Groups [421]

Age group	July 2004	July 2030
65–69 years	9,928,000	19,844,000
70–74 years	8,375,000	17,878,000
75–79 years	7,432,000	14,029,000
80–84 years	5,432,000	9,638,000
85–89 years	2,954,000	5,077,000
90–94 years	1,351,000	2,457,000
95–99 years	425,000	1,015,000
100 years and older	88,000	381,000

Twenty percent of people 65 and older (about 6 million) need some level of LTSS. The mean age is 80.5 years and the person is most likely to be a widowed white female. Forty percent who are living in the community are cognitively impaired, with Alzheimer's disease, mental retardation (7%), or senility, or have ADL needs. Forty percent living in the community have informal care, 25.1

percent have both informal and formal care, 4.6 percent have formal care, and 29.6 percent have care in an institution. [422]

The next few decades will bring an unprecedented increase in the size of the elderly population. Major factors to consider in predicting the impact of the aging population follow:

- The aging U.S. population, in particular the growth in the proportion of the people age 85 and over, will place increasing demands on our fragmented LTC system. The demands are uncertain.
- LTC will continue to be a woman's issue.
- The LTC population will become more ethnically diverse.
- Aging is not geographically uniform.
- Americans are unprepared to pay for LTC. [423]

Chronic Care Demographics

About 57 million working-age Americans, 18–64 years old, live with chronic disease conditions such as diabetes, asthma, or depression. In 2003, more than one in five (12.3 million) people with chronic diseases lived in families that had problems paying medical bills. [424]

Chronic diseases—such as cardiovascular disease (primarily heart disease and stroke), cancer, and diabetes—are among the most prevalent, costly, and preventable of all health problems. Seven of every 10 Americans who die each year (more than 1.7 million people) die of a chronic disease. Chronic disabling conditions cause major limitations in activity for more than 1 in every 10 Americans (25 million people). [425]

Eight of the top 10 causes of death in the United States in 1997 were due to chronic diseases: heart disease (31.4%), cancer (23.3%), stroke (6.9%), chronic obstructive pulmonary disease (4.7%), pneumonia/flu (3.7%), diabetes (2.7%), kidney disease (1.1%), chronic liver disease (1.1%). [426] Only unintentional injury (4.1%) and suicide (1.3%) are not related to chronic disease.

The main contribution to chronic disease is exposure to risk factors, such as tobacco use, unhealthful diets, lack of physical activity, and alcohol use. [427]

Estimates of chronic disease costs include the following:

- More than 90 million Americans have a chronic illness.
- Chronic diseases account for 70 percent of all deaths in the United States.

- Medical costs of people with chronic diseases account for more than 75 percent of the nation's $1.4 trillion medical care costs.
- Chronic diseases account for one-third of the years of life lost before age 65.
- The direct and indirect costs of diabetes are nearly $132 billion a year.
- Arthritis annually results in estimated medical care costs of more than $22 billion and estimated total costs (medical and lost productivity) of almost $82 billion.
- The estimated direct and indirect costs associated with smoking exceed $75 billion annually.
- In 2001, approximately $300 billion was spent on all cardiovascular diseases. Over $129 billion in lost productivity was due to cardiovascular disease.
- Direct medical costs associated with physical inactivity were nearly $76.6 billion in 2000. [428]

Despite annual spending of over $500 billion, half of the people with chronic illnesses do not receive appropriate care:

- 27% of individuals with hypertension (high blood pressure) are adequately treated;
- 50% of diabetics have controlled blood sugar, lipid, and blood pressure levels;
- 35% of eligible people with atrial fibrillation receive anticoagulation;
- 25% of people with depression are receiving adequate treatment;
- 44% of people with heart failure who experience a hospital stay are readmitted with the same problem within six months; [429]
- 50% of the elderly fail to receive pneumococcal vaccine; and
- 50% of heart attack victims fail to receive beta-blockers. [430]

A large study examined 439 indicators of 30 chronic diseases (6,712 people) in the United States. Findings showed that people received only 54.9 percent of scientifically indicated care. The study concluded that the "defect rate" in the quality of American health care is approximately 45 percent. Recommendations of the study were to clarify national goals for improvement, change the care delivery processes/systems, change the organizations that deliver care, and change the environment of professional medical practice. [431]

Another rationale for unmanaged chronic care was found in a study of 6.6 million uninsured people living with chronic conditions, with almost half reporting problems paying medical bills. Of the chronically ill with medical bill problems, 42 percent went without needed care, 65 percent delayed care, and 71 percent failed to get needed prescription drugs, all due to cost concerns. [432]

Between 2001 and 2003, the proportion of low-income chronically ill people with private insurance who spent more than 5 percent of their income on out-of-pocket health care costs grew from 28 percent to 42 percent, a 50 percent increase to 2.2 million people. [433]

Inequalities in income and education underlie many health disparities in the United States. They are intrinsically related and often serve as a proxy for each other. In general, population groups that suffer the worst health status and chronic disease morbidity/mortality are those that have the highest poverty rates and the least education. In 1996, the total number of whites below the poverty level was 12 percent, compared with African Americans (28 percent) and Hispanics (29 percent). [434]

According to a Kaiser Family Foundation survey in 2003, people with disabilities use the health care system frequently, with more than half (57%) having seen a physician four or more times in six months and 18 percent reporting two or more visits to the emergency room in the past six months. [435] While only 15 percent of the survey respondents say they have no regular doctor, one in four reports having trouble finding a doctor who understands his or her disability. When it comes to finding a doctor who accepts their insurance, 17 percent of the sample reported having had such problems, with higher rates reported by those covered by Medicaid. [436] Seventeen percent of those with a mental disability said the cost of mental health services is a serious problem for them. Prescription drug costs affected 32 percent of the respondents, and 36 percent of those taking prescription drugs admitted having skipped doses of the drug, split pills, or gone without filling a prescription. Twenty-one percent of the people who use equipment to manage their disability say they have serious difficulties paying for it. [437] Those with disabilities were less likely than the general population to receive preventive services and they received those services considerably less frequently than is generally recommended. Less than half of all female respondents reported having a mammogram in the past year, and only about a third of all men reported having a prostate examination. Only 41 percent reported having a dental examination in the past year. [438]

Racial and Ethnic Disparities

Healthy People 2010 cites race and ethnicity differences as a factor in chronic disease mortality and morbidity. The U.S. infant mortality rate is down, but the infant death rate among African Americans is still more than double that of whites. Heart disease rates are 40 percent higher for African Americans than for whites. The death rate for all cancers is 30 percent higher for African Americans compared with whites; for prostate cancer, it is more than double than for whites. The death rate from HIV/AIDS for African Americans is more than seven times than that for whites. Hispanics living in the United States are twice as likely to die from diabetes than non-Hispanic whites. Although constituting only 11 percent of the total population in 1996, Hispanics accounted for 20 percent of the new cases of tuberculosis. Puerto Ricans have a low infant birth-weight rate that is 50 percent higher than that for whites. Hispanics also have higher rates of high blood pressure and obesity than non-Hispanic whites. [439]

By 2050, people of color are expected to make up nearly half of the U.S. population. [440] A study analyzed data on 419,843 children 17 years and younger from 1979 to 2000 and found 22,758 with disabilities living in the community. [441] Disparities in the prevalence of ADL difficulties caused by chronic conditions or disability in the black and white non-Hispanic population were found to increase over time. Black children had higher prevalence rates in disability, due in part to differences in poverty status. The prevalence of difficulty with ADLs for white children increased over time to 47 percent—or 40.7 per 1,000 to 59.7 per 1,000 children in the population. For black children, the prevalence increased 77 percent—or 37.9 per 1,000 to 67.1 per 1,000 children in the population. Black children were 13 percent more likely than white children to have a reported activity limitation.

The prevalence of disability caused by chronic conditions has increased markedly for both black and white children. In the past, white children were in the mild chronic category. Researchers believe that the higher rates of disability are due, in part, to the increased exposure to poverty, racial disparities, lack of education, social opportunities, restricted access to care, increased exposure to environmental causes of disability, poor nutrition, and poor quality health care.

The death rate for 13 to 15 leading causes of death are higher and life expectancy is lower for black Americans than for white Americans. Asthma prevalence rates are higher for blacks, and there are more premature births and deaths in infancy.

The Kaiser Family Foundation reported nonelderly uninsured rates by race and ethnicity in 2003: 13 percent white; 20 percent Asian/Pacific Islander; 21

percent black; 28 percent American Indian and Native Alaskan; other, 1.8 percent; and 34 percent Latino. [442]

Combined, 36 percent of the 53 million Americans with disabilities are black and Latino (U.S. Census Bureau 2000). A recent GAO studied confirmed that the black population has higher disability rates, lower lifetime earnings, and shorter life expectancy than whites. [443] Sixteen percent of workers who are black die before the age of 62. Twenty-seventy percent of the Social Security Disability Insurance (SSDI) benefits are for the black and Latino population. The study found that people of color are receiving more public benefits over a lifetime then they contribute in payroll taxes. [444]

The demographic profile of individuals receiving both Medicaid and Medicare (7 million dual eligibles) shows that 4 million dual eligibles are mostly nonwhite widowed women over the age of 65 with multiple chronic disabilities. The dual eligible population is a major factor in the current problem, as it represents about 14 percent of the Medicaid population. In FY 2000, of the total Medicaid service spending of $168.1 billion, $70.8 billion or 42 percent was attributed to dual eligibles in payment for Medicaid covered benefits and in deductibles and coinsurance for Medicare services. [445]

Summary

If not addressed, the issues of poverty, lack of insurance, and continued segregation from affordable and consistent health care will increase the future needs and costs for LTSS. The increase in disability and prevalence in young black and white children cannot be ignored as we seek to design LTSS policy for the future. Despite disagreement among researchers, policymakers, and the consumer populations as to appropriate methods to define and determine which person with a disability has unmet needs, there is a common understanding that the number of people in need is growing at a rate that is far beyond current capacity of federal programs to respond.

The next section will provide an overview of the current pathways to LTSS for people with disabilities and the change in purpose, services, eligibility, and costs.

Part IV

LOWERING THE LIFEBOATS

Medicaid's expanding purposes, pathways, services, and costs for people with disabilities.

The grandfather of LTSS is Medicaid, [446] whose original purpose was to provide health care and nursing home care to very low-income families with dependent children, poor elderly, and disabled individuals. [447] The concept of LTC was not developed in the early years of Medicaid, and nursing home care represented the narrow scope of what it meant to age in America in the 1960s. Today, there are many additions to the original federal Medicaid purpose that reflect the growing trend for beneficiaries to receive services and supports in the home and the community and less in the nursing home. In FY 2003, 53.0 million Americans were enrolled in Medicaid, including 24.8 million children and 13.6 million aged, blind, or disabled individuals. [448] Total Medicaid assistance payments for FY 2002, not including administration, were "$246.3 billion and the four largest categories were: nursing facilities–19.3% of the total; inpatient services (general and mental hospitals)–14.3%; prepaid health care (capitation payments–managed care organizations)–13.3%; and prescription drugs–9.5%." [449]

The relevance and purpose of LTSS for Americans with disabilities has never been more important as the United States addresses its current social and fiscal obligation to meet the growing demands of an increased disability and aging population over the next century. The concept of LTSS for people with disabilities has evolved over the past 40 years as the expectations and image of people with disabilities has changed. Clearly, in order to work, people with lifelong impairments need access to affordable nonmedical supports and services, as well as ongoing reliable and affordable health care. For aging Americans with

disabilities, the same holds true—all need affordable supports and services and
health care to maintain dignity and independence.

State Medicaid programs receive their funding from federal Medicaid funds
that are not capped and rise to meet state Medicaid spending. The match from
federal Medicaid depends on a state's per capita income—the higher the income,
the lower the match. Nationally, the federal match pays for roughly 57 percent of
total Medicaid spending. [450] Geography plays an important role in the uneven
distribution of services and supports, because poorer states often have fewer
resources to spend, larger populations of seniors to serve, and higher disability
rates. [451] The menu of services under Medicaid is listed in state plans.
Mandatory services are services that all states opting to have a Medicaid program
must provide to all of their citizens. Optional services are additional and states can
limit the number of enrollees and services. [452, 453]

**Mandatory Medicaid services that all states must cover include the
following**: hospital care (inpatient and outpatient); physician services; laboratory
and X-ray services; family planning services; health center and rural health clinic
services; nurse midwife and nurse practitioner services; early and periodic
screening, diagnostic, and treatment (EPSDT) services and immunizations for
children under age 21; nursing home care; and home health services for those
eligible for nursing home care. [454]

Optional services that states may choose to cover include the following:
basic medical and health care services (including prescribed drugs); [455] services
that support people with disabilities to live in their communities, such as personal
care services (37 states offer personal care, 2003); rehabilitative and or clinic
services (29 states offer rehabilitative services, 2003); case management services
(49 states, 2003); and small group homes that operate as intermediate care
facilities for persons with mental retardation and developmental disabilities for 15
or fewer residents; aides, therapies, and related professional services. [456]
Services involving short- or long-term institutional stays include inpatient
psychiatric hospital services for children and young people under age 21; nursing
facility services for children and young people under age 21; ICF/MRs with more
than 15 residents; inpatient hospital services for people age 65 or older with
mental illness in institutions for mental diseases (IMDs); and nursing facility
services for people age 65 or older with mental illness in IMDs. [457]

Medicaid's purpose and scope and pathways to services grew and by the
1980s there were more than 50 distinct population groups wanting to become
eligible in states programs. [458] Many new eligibility pathways were added to
the Medicaid statute, including coverage of higher income children and pregnant
women as well as other elderly and disabled individuals. [459] Most recently, the

Medicaid statute allowed states to extend benefits to women with breast or cervical cancer, uninsured individuals with tuberculosis, immigrants (with certain conditions), and certain other working individuals with disabilities. [460] Today, more than one-third of Medicaid beneficiaries participate in new pathways added since the 1980s; the introduction of HCBS waivers and other programs has allowed for insurance coverage of vulnerable populations not previously eligible. [461]

In a 2005 report to the National Governors Association (NGA), researchers from Health Management Associates report that Medicaid's $300 billion program ($134 billion is for LTC programs) [462] has mushroomed into a constellation of several programs that include the following:

- an insurance program for low-income, uninsured children and some parents and pregnant women;
- a program of chronic care and LTC for people with disabilities, mental illness, and low-income elderly;
- a supplement to Medicare for low-income seniors and people with disabilities, and a support for those awaiting qualification for Medicare on the basis of permanent disability; and
- a source of funding for safety nets for hospitals and community health centers that serve a disproportionate share (DHS) of the uninsured. [463]

The report made the distinction that two-thirds of Medicaid spending is for population groups and services technically defined as optional and 90 percent of all LTC Medicaid services today fall under the optional category. [464] States are making cuts to many of the optional services as they struggle with the addition of 8.4 million beneficiaries and a one-third increase in program spending between 2000 and 2003. [465] In 2003, 49 states and the District of Columbia implemented Medicaid cuts, according to the Kaiser Commission on Medicaid and the Uninsured, and 32 states revisited their initial cuts and made more. Cost-containment measures implemented included the following: 37 states reduced or froze provider payments to hospitals and nursing homes; 45 states implemented prescription drug cost controls; 27 states report that they cut or restricted Medicaid eligibility; 25 states reduced benefits; and 17 states increased copayments. [466]

The Kaiser Commission Report added that a number of states were planning further cuts to their LTC spending and medically needy programs (allows individuals to "spend down" to qualify by reducing medical expenses from income) and that *any* cuts could affect access to health care for people with disabilities who rely mainly on Medicaid for a number of important services. [467] Reform proposals over the past few years have suggested federal caps for Medicaid spending that would eventually phase out optional services; these services would either be institutionalized by the states, and the costs absorbed, or they would no longer be offered due to lack of funds. Any cuts to the current menu of optional benefits would erode services and supports that are the lifeline for millions of low-income people with disabilities. [468, 469]

Low-income people with disabilities have benefited from the growing purpose of Medicaid and continue to enter the program through a complex mix of mandatory and optional pathways for eligibility. [470]

The following highlights of the mandatory and optional pathways that are specific to people with disabilities under Medicaid provide an overview of the programs, the states involved, and, in some instances, the costs.

Mandatory

- *Supplemental Security Income (SSI): This is a means-tested cash assistance, mandatory program for aged, blind, and disabled individuals* whose incomes are less than 74 percent of the federal poverty level. *One exception is the "209(b) option that allows states (about 11 states in 2004) to set eligibility standards that are more restrictive than current SSI standards,"* using SSI income, resource, and disability standards in place on January 2, 1972. Individuals who qualify for SSDI may also qualify for Medicaid. [471]
- *Qualified Medicare Beneficiary (QMB): This applies to certain low-income individuals (<100% of poverty) who have disabilities as defined under SSI and who are eligible for Medicare cost-sharing expenses paid by Medicaid.* Medicaid pays Medicare Part B premiums, deductibles, and coinsurance for Medicare-covered benefits but no Medicaid benefits unless individuals qualify for Medicaid through other eligibility pathways (e.g., via SSI, medically needy, or the special income rule.)
- *Specified Low-Income Beneficiary: This applies to individuals who are eligible for Medicare cost-sharing and whose incomes are less than 100–120 percent of poverty.* Medicaid pays Medicare Part B premium.

Optional [472]

- *State Supplemental Payment (SSP) benefits with state-only dollars* on a monthly basis help cover items such as food, shelter, clothing utilities, and other daily necessities. SSI applicants must be allowed to deduct medical expenses from their income when determining financial eligibly for Medicaid. This is sometimes referred to as "spend down" and is critical to working people with disabilities. (In October 2001, 21 states reported providing this coverage to people with disabilities and 3 states provided this coverage only to people who are blind.) [473]
- *Omnibus Budget Reconciliation Act of 1986 offered states an option for covering people whose income exceeds SSI or 209(b) levels up to 100 percent of the federal poverty level.* In 2003, 20 states and the District of Columbia used this option.
- *Special income rule, the "300 percent" rule,* allows states to extend Medicaid to certain individuals with incomes too high to qualify for SSI, but who are eligible for nursing facility or other institutional care. The Miller Trust allows applicants under this rule to place income in excess of the special income level into a trust, making the state the beneficiary after death.
- *Medically Needy Program* extends Medicaid coverage beyond the aged and people with disabilities to families with children who do not meet the applicable income (or resource) requirements for other eligibility pathways. States may set their medically need monthly limits for a family of a given size at any level up to 133 1/3 percent of the former AFDC (now TANF) program standard. (In FY 2003, 35 states and the District of Columbia had medically needy programs, and 33 of these programs were extended to people age 65 and older and people with disabilities.)
- *Rules for working people with disabilities on SSI* are linked to an individual's ability to work and earn income and "engage in substantial gainful activity" (SGA). A person is considered able to engage in SGA if his or her earnings exceed $830 per month for 2005; $1,380 for people who are blind. Under a waiver called 1619(a), SSI law permits states that extend Medicaid to SSI working recipients to receive Medicaid even when they are working above the SGA level. As an individual's earnings increase, his or her cash benefits are gradually reduced through a special income disregard formula. [474]

- *Ticket to Work and Work Incentives Improvement Act of 1999 (TWIIA)*
  allows states to raise their Medicaid income and asset limits for
  individuals with disabilities who work. States may require that working
  individuals with disabilities "buy-in" to the Medicaid program by sharing
  in the costs of their coverage. *Medicaid buy-in* allows states to expand
  Medicaid coverage to working individuals with disabilities between the
  ages of 16 and 34, with incomes and resources as defined by the state,
  and allows states to impose premiums and other cost-sharing on
  individuals who qualify (in 2002, 25 states). [475] *Under TWIIA, the*
  medical improvement group option targets individuals with cyclical or
  periodic disabilities who are working at the federal minimum wage at
  least 40 hours a month or who meet other definitions approved by HHS.
  Three states currently participate in this option: Connecticut, Indiana, and
  Missouri. [476]
- *Katie Beckett Option* allows children to stay in their homes who would
  otherwise be institutionalized, and parents' income are not attributed (21
  states have this option). Tax Equity and Fiscal Responsibility Act 1982.
- *Home- and Community-Based Service Waivers* allow states, through a
  waiver process, to provide at-risk individuals with services at home (49
  states use HCBS waivers, introduced in 1981 and currently serving
  almost 1 million Americans.) The federal HCBS waiver authorized by
  Congress in 1981 is the principal Medicaid program that underwrites
  LTSS for the MR/DD population in the United States. Federal spending
  for HCBS grew for MR/DD from $1.2 billion in 1982 to $7.2 billion in
  2002. The average state ICF/MR cost in 2002 was $134,619 per resident
  per year, compared with the HCBS cost per participant of $35,215. [477]
  The waiver provides the financing mechanism for states to expand their
  menu of community supports that promote economic independence and
  self-sufficiency for people with MR/DD. State data revealed that by 2002
  all states but Mississippi were spending more for community services
  than for institutional services. [487] In 2002, national spending for
  MR/DD was $34.6 billion, and combined individual and family support
  spending of $4.4 billion constituted 13 percent of nationwide funding; 53
  percent was allotted for supported living and personal assistance; 32
  percent for family support, and the remaining 15 percent funded
  supported employment activities. [479] For FY 2003, HCBS increased
  9.3 percent from $16.9 billion to $18.6 billion. [480] Three-fourths of
  HCBS waivers (nearly $14.0 billion) are used to purchase LTSS for
  people with MR/DD. [481] The other 25 percent of waiver expenditures

were for people with physical disabilities and older people and totaled $4.2 billion in FY 2003: Brain injuries accounted for $163 million (a 59% increased from FY 2002); HIV or AIDS and technology-dependent or medically fragile people accounted for an additional 0.9 percent of all waiver spending (about $167 million in FY 2003). There were three small waiver programs, which served individuals with a primary diagnosis of mental illness, accounting for 0.2 percent of HCBS waiver expenditures. [482]

- *Family Support Services* for MR/DD consist of any community-based services administered or financed by the state MR/DD agency that provide "vouchers, direct cash payments to families, reimbursement, or direct payments to service providers which the state agency identified as family support." [483] Examples of family supports are "cash subsidy payments, respite care, family counseling, architectural adaptation of the home, in-home training, sibling support programs, education and behavior management services, and the purchase of specialized equipment." [484] All 50 states reported a family support initiative in 2002 (the District of Columbia did not provide a family support initiative).

- *Supported Employment* began in the early 1980s as long-term support for workers with developmental disabilities to enhance and supplement the states' vocational rehabilitation services already in place. Supported employment refers to "small business enterprise, work crews, enclaves within industry and individual job placements." [485] The research in this field overwhelmingly shows that people with developmental disabilities want paid jobs in the community. In 2002, 24 percent of all vocational and day program participants in the United States worked in supported or competitive employment and the other 76 percent received services in sheltered employment, day activity, or day habilitation programs. States spent $662,768,320 in 2002 on supported employment for 112,417 MR/DD participants. [486] HCBS waiver spending for supported employment grew since the Balanced Budget Act of 1997 removed the requirement that HCBS-supported employment participants be previously institutionalized.

- *Supported Living* for MR/DD is "housing in which individuals with MR/DD choose to live and ownership is by someone other than the support provider and the individual has an individualized support plan." Forty-seven states reported providing supported living services to 95,223 individuals in 2002, at a cost of $2.0 billion. The national average for supported living was $20,643, with a range of $2,196 in Mississippi to $124,544 in Oklahoma. [487]

- **_Personal Assistance_** is "support provided to people living in their own homes financed by either state funds or federal/state Medicaid funds and defined by the state as 'personal assistance.'" [488] In 2002, for MR/DD, 22 states had initiatives with combined supported living and personal assistance spending of $2.3 billion, which constituted 7 percent of the total MR/DD spending. Expenditure data ranged from $844 in West Virginia to $89,354 in Oklahoma, with a national average of $14,146. [489] The Federal Government has encouraged supported living through legislation: The Medicaid Community Supported Living Arrangement (CSLA) legislation enacted in 1990 endorsed supported living principles and provided funding for eight states to establish statewide supported living initiatives.

Medicaid spending for acute care and LTC combined in 2002 was $91,889 billion for the blind/disabled category compared with $51,733 billion for the aged, $31,247 billion for children, $23,493 billion for adults, and $4,282 billion for foster care children. [490] Spending for the aged was higher in two service categories compared with the same two service categories for the blind/disabled: (1) LTSS spending for the aged was $35,242 billion versus $29,554 billion for the blind/disabled; (2) nursing facility services spending for the aged was $30,002 billion versus $8,770 billion for the blind/disabled. Personal support services were higher for the blind/disabled—$8,262 billion compared with $3,505 billion for the aged. [491] The aged and blind/disabled categories combined represent 15 percent of the total Medicaid population.

Summary

The growth of eligibility pathways for Medicaid beneficiaries with disabilities and the rising costs reflect the intense needs of its major beneficiaries: people with mental retardation and developmental disabilities. Reform efforts to date have been incremental and represent the path of least resistance. As the country ages and more people enter Medicaid, it is unclear how the current fiscal safety net for the MR/DD population can be sustained by states that will be addressing the additional costs of prescription drug benefits as well. [492]

The changes to the Medicaid program have become the path of least resistance for incremental reform. Part V will describe the many challenges in forecasting future demographic trends and gaps in services and supports.

Part V

APPROACHING THE ICEBERG

Economic and Financial Challenges to Reform

Global Challenges

The current agenda for 21st century Americans with disabilities must include a clear examination of how aging (both at home and abroad) will affect the economic well-being of people with disabilities to live fully independent and meaningful lives. A 2005 report by McKinsey & Company found that aging will cause a global wealth shortfall over the next two decades and that growth in household financial wealth will slow by more than two-thirds (from 4.5 percent historically to 1.3 percent going forward), with the United States the largest source of the global shortfall ($19 trillion) because of its dominant share of global wealth. [493] Left unchecked, this trend "could significantly reduce future economic and health care needs of aging populations." [494]

The staff at the International Monetary Fund in January 2004 reported that the growing imbalance between what the U.S. Government has promised to pay in future benefits and its expected revenues would require "an immediate and permanent 60 percent hike in the federal income tax, or a 50 percent cut in Social Security and Medicare benefits." [495] Many federal reports confirm the growing fiscal insolvency of these programs, using different economic models and projections of costs, and all agree that the current growth is unsustainable. [496, 497]

> Public solutions that focus on limiting
> public obligation for LTC financing do
> our nation a disservice.
>
> *Dr. Judy Feder, April, 19, 2005*
> *Testimony U.S. Congress on LTC*

America is also highly dependent on foreign capital and is currently importing far more goods and services than it is exporting; it is becoming more indebted to foreign countries. [498] Western Europe and Japan are aging more rapidly than the United States and may need additional capital to finance their own growing deficits. The growing global debt due to the war on terror and other factors combined with the rising costs for health care and the growing number of seniors without sufficient retirement income to cover their LTC responsibilities place major pressure on current federal programs like Medicaid.

In his forward to Jeffrey Sachs' book *The End of Poverty—Economic Possibilities for Our Time*, Bono wrote that America "can be the generation that no longer accepts that an accident of latitude determines whether a child lives or dies—but will we be that generation?" Sachs' premise is that we can end poverty in the world in this generation if we choose, and he lays out an extraordinary plan to do so. America has its own poverty right now and, although it is much unlike the extreme poverty Bono and Sachs talk about, these Americans are in need of their own champions and a plan. People with disabilities are the poorest of the poor—among working adults, "nearly 40% of people with disabilities have family incomes less than 200% of poverty compared to 22% of the non-disabled." [499]

As discussed in chapter 1, the United States is a noncontender in the life expectancy race compared with other countries that spend much less per capita. The World Health Organization's (WHO) Disability-Adjusted Life Expectancy measure is used to examine health data in every nation in the world, starting with life expectancy then subtracting years of ill health after weighting the level and duration of each disability. [500] In the 2000 survey, the United States came in 24th for life expectancy at 70 years. The survey found that Americans die earlier and spend more time disabled than people in most other industrialized countries. One WHO executive said that "portions of our population are very poor and suffer from the poor health more characteristic of a poor developing country rather than a rich industrialized one." [501]

The disparities in health outcomes and disability are increasing for Americans under age 65 because of poverty, rising rates of obesity and diabetes, and increased longevity for individuals with lifelong disabilities, such as Down syndrome and mental retardation. The disparity in poverty rates is evident among seniors: 8.3 percent of whites live in poverty compared with 22.7 percent of black seniors and 20.4 percent of Hispanic seniors. The highest poverty rate (58.8%) is experienced by older Latino women who live alone. [502]

Healthy People 2010 estimated that direct medical and indirect annual costs associated with disability are more than $300 billion, or 4 percent of the gross domestic product (GDP). This total cost includes $160 billion in medical care expenditures (1994 dollars) and lost productivity approaching $155 billion. [503]

Federal Roles in Financing LTSS

Medicare and Medicaid programs are the fastest growing entitlement programs and together account for 62.5 percent of the $151.2 billion spent on LTSS in 2001. [504] Medicaid's federal share as a percentage of GDP will grow from today's 1.5 percent to 2.6 percent in 2035 and 4.8 percent in 2080. [505] Medicare's federal share will triple as a share of GDP from 2.7 percent to 7.5 percent by 2035 and reach 13.8 percent in 2080. Social Security spending will grow as a federal share of the GDP from 4.3 percent today to 6.3 percent in 2035 and will reach 6.4 percent in 2080. Combined, all three programs are projected to double by 2035. [506] If the current federal health and retirement programs continue to grow at these rates, by 2040 federal revenues will be adequate to pay little more than interest on the federal debt. [507] By 2010, the share of the population age 65 and older will begin to climb, with profound implications: Social Security and Medicare (the Hospital Insurance portion) are pay-as-you-go programs—as the ratio of workers to retirees declines, so will the income for these programs. [508]

The GAO report also found that the prevalence of disability will go up, although it has had a steady decline over the past 16 years (it was noted earlier that the reasons may be environmental rather then health-related.) In 2000, one in five adults had unmet needs for LTSS. That need is expected to double by 2020.

States do not have the fiscal capacity to assume the primary role for their aging and disability populations without significant federal participation. The following data describes how integral the federal role is in partnership with states to finance current LTSS:

- *Of the $1.24 trillion spent on all U.S. personal health care services in 2001, $151.2 billion (12 percent) was spent on LTSS.* [509]
- *Total Medicaid Spending for acute care and LTSS in 2003 was $276.1 billion and exceeded net outlays for Medicare.* [510] *The federal share for Medicaid in 2003 was $161.0.*
- *Total spending for LTSS was $150.2 billion in 2001; Medicaid financed 48 percent, or $73.1 billion, of the federal share,* with 64.3 percent covering care in nursing facilities and ICF/MRs and the balance spent on HCBS. The national average Medicaid nursing home payment is $97 per day or $2,942 per month. There is variation by state; for example, Florida has an average monthly Medicaid nursing home cost of $3,496 compared with Iowa's average monthly cost of $2,275. The average U.S. annual cost of assisted living is $28,548. [511]
- *Medicare financed 18.0 percent, or $33 billion, of total LTC expenditures in 2003,* with 54 percent for skilled nursing facility care and the balance for home health care. [512]
- *Families and individuals financed 20 percent, or $38 billion, of out-of-pocket expenditures in 2003,* mostly for nursing home care (82%). [513] In the early 1960s, nearly half of health care spending was financed by individuals, with the rest provided by public programs and health insurance. [514] By 2002, individual out-of-pocket spending at the point of service was estimated to be 14 percent. [515]
- *Donated care represented 36 percent of LTSS care in 2004, at a cost estimated between $103 and $218 billion.* [516] Using the $218 billion estimate, this represented approximately $24,000 per senior.
- *Private LTC insurance represented 9.6 percent ($16 billion) of all U.S. spending on LTC insurance in 2003,* with 52 percent for nursing home care and the balance for home health care. [517]
- *Other federal programs provided 5.9 percent, or $151.2 billion,* for 2001 and included the Older Americans Act and the Social Services Block Grant (SSBG) program (Title XX of the Social Security Act), both of which fund a variety of community-based services. In 2001, the Older Americans Act was amended to authorize the National Family Caregiver Support Program (NFCSP), which offers assistance to family caregivers of the frail elderly. Some states supplement SSI to help low-income individuals pay for HCBS or to reside in nonmedical residential settings such as board and care homes. Certain programs under the Rehabilitation Act of 1973 provide a range of supportive services to people with

disabilities. The Department of Veteran Affairs (VA) provides a wide range of LTC services to the nation's veterans that include nursing home, domiciliary, home health care, and assistance to caregivers. Tax benefits for LTC include a limited deduction for LTC expenses and insurance premiums, tax-exempt insurance benefits, and the dependent care tax credit. [518]

GAO, in "21st Century Challenges: Reexamining the Base of the Federal Government," provided policymakers and government agencies with a compendium of areas considered ripe for review and reexamination, along with a framework for evaluating and identifying the issues and solutions. Question 4 of the GAO framework concerns affordability and cost-effectiveness. If we inserted LTSS into the formula, this is how the questions would look: [519]

- Are LTSS affordable and financially sustainable over the long term, given known cost trends, risks, and future fiscal imbalances?
- Is LTSS using the most cost-effective or net beneficial approaches when compared to other tools and program designs?
- What would be the likely consequences of eliminating the program, policy, function, or activity?
- What would be the likely implications if its total funding is cut by 25 percent?

It is clear from the research that the current funding mechanisms to support LTSS (primarily coming from Medicaid) are exceeding states' capacity and still not providing many of the services needed for a growing younger and older population that is not MR/DD or on Medicaid. In addition to the patchwork system of publicly financed LTSS, private LTC insurance is an alternative financing strategy.

Medicaid and Private Insurance

The sources for individual health care coverage for the elderly and people with disabilities are Medicare, Medicaid, and private insurance. All health care coverage plans have certain covered services and gaps in coverage. The type of health care coverage determines access to the kind of care and services and supports people with a disability over and under age 65 receive. Each health care coverage plan covers different services and different populations.

Medicaid provides coverage for most medical services, mental health care, LTC, and prescription drugs. The single benefit used by the largest number of Medicaid recipients is prescription drugs. In FY 2002, 24.4 million Medicaid beneficiaries used this benefit, followed by physician services, which were used by 22.1 million recipients. [520] (The prescription drug benefit will shift to Medicare in 2006, and it is unclear what the impact of this change will be for people with disabilities, particularly those receiving both Medicare and Medicaid.) [521]

Fourteen percent of the U.S. population (40.8 million) used Medicaid and the State Children's Health Insurance Program (SCHIP) in 2001 as their primary source of health insurance. [522] Enrollees are described as "heterogeneous" in terms of the duration of their enrollment and the extent to which they rely on Medicaid and SCHIP as their sole source of coverage.

The CRS described three distinct groups using Medicaid and SCHIP in 2001: [523]

- *18.8 million relied solely on both Medicaid and SCHIP for the entire year;* 69 percent were children under age 19 and none were aged.
- *12.3 million used both Medicaid and SCHIP for part of the year* and were uninsured for two-thirds of the months they spent without Medicaid/SCHIP. Job-based health insurance covered nearly all of the remaining months; 1.8 million experienced a loss of job-based coverage during the year, and 61 percent were linked to policyholders (spouse or parent) who experienced substantial disruption in their employment and insurance status. An additional 14 percent were linked to policyholders who were employed but experienced a drop in wages. [524]
- *9.7 million never relied solely on Medicaid* during the year and had other sources of coverage; under 23 percent were children, but nearly half (46%) were aged. [525]

The report highlights the common theme of poverty across these three groups, as well as differences by race. Thomas Shapiro found that two out of every five American families do not have enough money to live at the poverty line for three months and defines this phenomenon as being "asset poor." [526] Fifty-four percent of black families are asset poor compared with 26 percent of white families. It is estimated that only 7 percent of American seniors have enough resources for one year of nursing home care, [527] and that cost of care is 20 percent higher in urban areas than in rural areas. In New York, California, and

Massachusetts, the cost of urban care was found to be 40 percent higher than in nonurban areas. [528]

The demographics of the Medicaid insured population, when broken into the three categories above, suggest a high vulnerability to rising health care costs and dependence on family members (69% of 12.8 million children) for coverage. The growth in spending and enrollment is due in part to downturns in the economy; the increase in health premiums (in 2001, job-based health insurance premiums increased by 10.9% while workers' earnings and overall inflation increased by less than half that amount); and the availability of expanded covered under public programs like Medicaid/SCHIP. [529]

The Economic and Social Research Institute found that nearly 49 percent of the uninsured are either self-employed or work at firms with fewer than 25 workers or for companies with fewer than 10 employees, of which only 52 percent offer insurance. [530] Over 50 percent of low-income employees of small firms with incomes below 200 percent of the federal poverty level are uninsured. [531] A 1999 report of the President's Advisory Commission, "Consumer Protection and Quality in the Health Care Industry," found that 600,000 of the 2 million health care paraprofessionals (nursing aides, home health aides, and home care aides) do not work full time and receive benefits and report wages below the poverty line. [532] (For an in-depth review, see "Supply and Demand Puzzle" in this section.)

Private Insurance

Over 6 million Americans own LTC insurance (about 10% of the U.S. population) and 50 percent of the claims paid are for Alzheimer's and other forms of dementia. [533] Genworth Financials (which provides LTC to 15 million customers in 22 countries) reports that cognitive claims since 1993 have increased 35 percent and that the annual dollar amount paid out has experienced a twelvefold increase, reaching approximately $120 million for cognitive care claims in 2003. [534] The allocation of cognitive claims was noted as moving from nursing homes to home health care and assisted living facilities.

Thomas Stinson, CEO of Genworth Financials, has more than 30 years of experience in the LTC insurance business. In his testimony before Congress, he reported that the average age of people buying LTC insurance has shifted dramatically from postretirement to preretirement—from age 69 to age 59. [535] Ten percent of those age 65 and older entering nursing homes will be there for five years or more, with average costs for 2004 at $179 per day; assisted living facilities cost $79 per day; and certified home care is about $20 per hour. The top 13 companies providing LTC insurance had paid out $8 billion in claims through 2002 and offer policies to individuals ranging in age from 18 to 99; they provide a $50 to $600 per day benefit. [536] Stinson confirmed what many studies have reported (see chapter 1, public opinion): that many Americans underestimate the financial risks involved with aging and do not understand the limits of Medicare. The focus of Stinson's testimony to Congress was on the aging population and not the specific needs of people with disabilities under the age of 65. However, the fact that 50 percent of LTC policies are covering cognitive claims suggests that more research is needed on the type of insurance coverage required by people under age 65.

State Partnerships for Long-Term Care and Medicaid

The National Association of Health Underwriters (NAHU) was represented at the April 19, 2005, hearing of the U.S. House of Representatives Ways and Means Committee on Long-Term Care; association representatives testified that 8 out of 10 people in America are not insured for the catastrophic expense of nursing home care (currently estimated at $70,000 annually). [537] Janet Trautwein of NAHU testified that the LTC partnership programs currently being offered in several states provide incentives for individuals who purchase private insurance and exhaust their benefits provided by the LTC insurance partnership policy to receive Medicaid as the payer for their LTC expenses. Policyholders are allowed to keep personal assets equal to the benefits paid by the original LTC policy. Mark Meiners also testified at this hearing that the partnership program can save Medicaid costs and that projected potential savings by 2017–2020 would produce a 7 percentage point decline in Medicaid's share of the LTC bill. [538] Current savings are in the range of $8 to $10 million. [539]

Disability Insurance

The lack of disability insurance was described as the "missing piece in the financial security puzzle" for Americans with disabilities and is an indication that the public underestimates the risk of having a disability. [540] The Task Force for the Disability Chart Book found the following:

- The risk of a disability during a worker's career is significant, as are the consequences to the individual and family financial security. (The increase in SSDI beneficiaries confirms this first finding.) [541, 542]
- The risk of disability is higher than premature death and is higher for older people than younger people, and females are more likely to become disabled than males. The majority of disabilities are caused by illnesses and not serious accidents (p. 4).
- Females have the highest risk of disability at age 35, at 29 percent, compared with a 20 percent risk for males (p. 7).
- The financial risk of disability is great and stops income and prevents retirement savings. A 45-year-old, currently earning $50,000 per year and suffering a permanent disability, could lose $1,000,000 in future earnings (p. 13).
- The public may overestimate the help that is available from public disability insurance programs (SSDI and other state-mandated, short-term programs provide a safety net but do not ensure financial security). Workers compensation benefits cover only disabilities caused by injury or illness arising on the job—only an estimated 4 percent of long-term disabilities. The SSDI definition for disability excludes many workers who qualify for private disability benefits (p. 29). [543]

Supply and Demand Puzzle

The issues of identification of current and projected future costs of an LTSS system are further complicated by the role of informal caregiving. There are no agreed-upon definitions for caregivers for the elderly and people with disabilities, especially when they are family and friends. Little consensus exists among the states about the recognition of families as a central component of the LTC system, such as in state statutes, in other state policies, or in the provision of other home- and community-based care programs and services. Providing explicit support to family and friends of frail elders represents a paradigm shift. Viewing the family caregiver as a "consumer" or "client" is a relatively new concept for many state agencies. [544]

Many policymakers and states disagree about whether family and informal caregivers should be considered clients or consumers in the LTC system and whether they should have access to their own support services. [545] Yet, according to the Kaiser Family Foundation Survey, only 8 percent of people with disabilities turn to professional sources for assistance, such as home health aides and personal assistants. Two-thirds rely on family members and friends as an important source of support. [546]

According the National Alliance for Caregiving and AARP, 44.4 million American caregivers age 18 and older provide unpaid care to an adult age 18 or older. Six out of 10 of those caregivers either work or have worked while providing care. Eighty-three percent are caring for a relative. Most of the caregivers (69%) are women. Most of the people receiving caregiving are women (65%) who are widowed (42%). Most care recipients are 50 years old or older (80%) and live in their own home. The typical caregiver is a 46-year-old woman who has at least some college experience and provides unpaid care to a widowed woman age 50 or older. [547]

The middle-aged women who currently provide much of the care, both formally and informally, will decrease in relative number, creating a situation in which the demand for LTC workers could substantially outstrip the supply. [548]

The most frequently reported unmet needs for caregivers are finding time for themselves (35%), managing emotional and physical stress (29%), and balancing work and family responsibilities (29%). To cope, 73 percent of caregivers say praying helps them with the caregiving stress, 61 percent talk with or seek advice from friends and relatives, and 44 percent say they read about caregiving in books. [549]

Family members and other informal caregivers, such as friends and neighbors, are the backbone of the LTC system, providing largely unpaid assistance to loved ones with chronic illnesses and disabilities. Without question, the economic value of family care is staggering. In 1998, HHS estimated that replacing donated LTC services for seniors with professional care would cost between $50 billion and $103 billion. Another recent analysis estimated the value of informal care of impaired people of all ages in 1997—measuring it as forgone wages of the caregiver—at $196 billion. [550] At an estimated value of $257 billion nationally (in 2000 dollars), informal caregiving greatly surpasses the costs associated with home health care ($32 billion) and nursing home care ($92 billion). [551]

The Older Americans Act of 2000 authorized NFCSP as a national program with the following support to caregivers:

- information to caregivers about available services;
- assistance to caregivers in gaining access to supportive services;
- individual counseling, support groups, and caregiving training to assist caregivers in making decisions and solving problems related to their role;

- respite care to temporarily relieve caregivers from their responsibilities; and
- supplemental services, on a limited basis, to complement care provided by caregivers. [552]

While this legislation offers new resources for caregivers, more research is needed to learn more about the programs that some states have designed and their impact and cost savings.

While caregiving by family and friends is ancient, it is not fully understood. The term "caregiver" needs to be defined. Caregiver prevalence studies should use the same definitions and parameters to gather better information. Issues such as caregiver training, caregiver burden and stress, negative impact on the physical health of caregivers, services they provide, and the economic impact of caregiving, especially the impact on work, need to be understood. [553] Outcomes and costs for caregiving and quality measures for the safety and health of the care recipient would address the value and gaps in caregiving.

Workforce Shortage and Recruitment and Retention Challenges

The demand for LTSS is growing. The cost is growing. The supply of paid workers, skilled and unskilled, to respond to the market demand is declining. The challenge for policymakers is not only to focus on workforce shortages and related costs of education, training, wages, and benefits but also to solve the puzzle of the role and relationship of informal caregiving to paid providers. Who is going to meet the growing demand for providing services and supports as informal caregiving decreases?

The workforce shortage is both a supply and demand problem. As the aging of the baby boom generation increases seniors' share of the population from 12.6 percent in 2000 to 20.5 percent in 2040, the demand for LTC services is virtually certain to increase. The population's aging will also cause a decline in the share of the population that is of a working age. In 2000, the ratio of people of working age to people of retirement age was 4.7. In 2040, the ratio is forecast to fall to 2.6. [554] There will be a shortage of workers and taxpayers, along with an increasing demand for health care services. It is not simply a supply-and-demand issue. Other issues affect the shortage, such as wages and the job itself.

As with most health care professions, there is a shortage of nurses and home care workers for LTC. As of 2002, the health care workforce included nearly 2.2 million registered nurses (RNs), about 700,000 licensed practical nurses (LPNs), and about 3.1 million paraprofessional workers, including nurse home health, personal care aides, and home care aides. The Health Resources and Services Administration forecast projects that the demand for RNs and LPNs in nursing homes will increase by 44.2 percent and 47.9 percent, respectively, between 2000 and 2020. The demand for RNs and LPNs in home health agencies is expected to increase by 43.8 percent and 53.8 percent, respectively, during the same period. According to the Bureau of Labor Statistics (BLS), jobs for nurses aides are also expected to grow by 23.8 percent, while the employment of personal care and home health aides could grow at a much more rapid rate of 58.1 percent between 1998 and 2008. [555] These statistics do not count the "gray market"—workers hired and supervised by consumers who pay for their own care, whose numbers are thought to be substantial. [556] This sector of paraprofessionals in the home— the home care worker—is consistently in BLS estimates of the top 20 fastest and largest job growth occupations. Over a half million new home care jobs will be created by 2012. [557]

This shortage in workers is occurring as the baby boomers age and the incidence of chronic disease is on the rise. The basic argument is that the aging of the baby boomers over the next few decades, along with improvements in longevity generated by medical advances, will cause a dramatic increase in the elderly population requiring LTC. [558] Government estimates suggest that the number of people using paid LTC services—in a nursing facility, alternative residential care facility such as assisted living, or at home—could nearly double, increasing from 15 million in 2000 to 27 million in 2050. [559] In the future, the labor force, on the whole, will not be growing as fast as either the LTC population or the population at greatest risk of needing LTC (i.e., people age 85 or older). [560]

Economists generally believe that market forces tend to eliminate shortages in the labor market (or elsewhere), especially with the passage of time. If wages and benefits are free to adjust, worker shortages in the short term should lead to higher compensation levels in a given market, which then should attract workers to that field and thereby ease the shortage. However, a number of factors might limit the speed of any such adjustment. [561] Factors may include competition for these workers, content of the job, conditions of work, and the ability to increase wages.

In particular, the shortage in direct care workers (paraprofessionals, nursing assistants, personal and home care aides, and home health aides) will have the greatest impact on community and home-based LTSS. The profile of the direct care worker is a woman who is 37 to 41 years old. Slightly over half of the direct care workers are white and non-Hispanic. About one-third are African American and the rest are Hispanic or other ethnicities. One-fourth of direct care workers are unmarried and living with children, compared with 11 percent of the total U.S. workforce. Two-fifths (41%) have completed their formal education with a high school diploma or general education diploma (GED). Another 38 percent have attended college. [562]

There is a shortage of direct care workers. Direct care work is unattractive in the LTC and health care sectors, and in the overall workforce, for many reasons. The content of the job and conditions of work may be one factor. In particular, care for the elderly may not be considered appropriate or appealing work for other potential labor pools, such as less-skilled men, and stressful work conditions might limit other potential candidates as well. [563] Another indicator is the high staff turnover in the LTC sector. Studies have found that the turnover rate in nursing facilities is nearly 100 percent for nursing aides. Home care agencies have annual turnover rates between 40 percent and 60 percent. [564] Possible explanations for the high turnover rates among nursing personnel in the LTC sector include relatively low wages, limited or no benefits, and greater physical and emotional exertion than is required in many other jobs in the health care sector. [565]

The wages are low. In 2003, the median hourly wage for all direct care workers was $9.20, significantly less than the median wage of $13.53 for all U.S. workers. Almost a fifth of direct care workers—far more than the national average of 12 percent to 13 percent—earn incomes below the poverty level, and 30 to 35 percent of all nursing home and home health aides who are single parents receive food stamps. [566] The financial ability for this sector to generate higher wages and benefits will be limited by the constraints on third-party payers, such as Medicaid and Medicare, which are and will continue to be pressured to reduce costs under the weight of a growing retirement population. [567]

There is little access to health benefits for the direct care worker, because the work is part time or the worker is self-employed. Home health aides average 29.2 hours per week, and nursing aides, orderlies, and attendants average 32 hours. [568] Because the work is part time, the worker often has to patch together a few jobs to make ends meet. In 1999, one-third (32.1%) of home care aides and one-fourth (25.2%) of certified nursing assistants in nursing homes had no health insurance, compared with one-sixth (16%) of all U.S. workers. [569]

The elasticity of the labor supply reflects the responsiveness of workers in any sector to the wages offered in that sector. A fairly elastic labor supply indicates that workers will respond in large numbers to higher wages. [570] Again, wages will not be the only factor that affects the transition of workers to LTC. If the willingness of people to work in LTSS depends heavily on the extent to which they enjoy providing care to the elderly; or if less-skilled men and other demographic groups (such as youth or the near-elderly) are not amenable to providing such work or view it as less prestigious or as a low-status occupation, the elasticity of the labor market for this sector will be relatively low. [571]

The following are other variables that shift the labor supply and that vary from state to state:

- Labor market demographics: This includes the population from which the LTC workers is typically drawn. The share of the population composed of less-educated (with a high school diploma or less) middle-aged women and/or immigrants.
- Unemployment rate: The local unemployment rate should also affect the relative supply to the LTC industry, as it reflects the amount of competition available from other low-wage occupations.
- Low-wage worker policies: Polices to improve the wages and benefits of low-wage workers overall should have some positive effects on the labor supply to the LTC sector. These policies might include state minimum wages above the national level, federal and state-earned income tax credits, or a generous SCHIP.
- Long-term support worker policies: Regulations might limit the supply of workers by imposing training or other requirements that make it harder to generate LTC workers. On the other hand, innovative recruitment or training programs could have more positive effects.
- Wages and employment in competing occupations/industries: Wages in competing sectors, such as hospitality and child care, are important for determining the potential willingness of workers to enter the long-term services sector from these other sectors. [572]

The issues for direct care workers and the labor supply must be understood on the national, state, and local levels. Among the top issues to be addressed are salary, full-time work, and benefits, balanced with long-term service funding for Medicare and Medicaid. For the success of consumer-directed programs and other Medicaid waiver programs, the workforce issues and shortages need to be resolved.

Summary

The documented growing demand for LTSS in the home and community raise new questions for researchers and policymakers about current costs and projected future costs for the under- and over-65 populations with disabilities. The cost conundrum is further exacerbated by four important factors.

First, insufficient data is available on LTSS costs for individuals across the spectrum of disabilities under age 65. Second, there is insufficient data on the costs of responding to a decreasing population of informal caregivers and the development of an appropriately trained and paid workforce. Third, there is a lack of agreement on the role and responsibility of the government versus individuals and families to cover the costs of current and future LTSS needs. Without research to explore different public and private cost-sharing scenarios, particularly for the under-65 population with disabilities, it would be difficult to explore the relationship of public financing and private insurance.

The fourth and final factor transcends the specific challenges of development of a responsive LTSS system for the targeted population. The global economic picture and changing demographics, in addition to the current federal budget deficit, raise questions about the political will to maintain current entitlements, let alone craft a new system.

Part VI

REVIEWING THE PASSENGER MANIFEST

Case studies of the costs and services and supports for six individuals with disabilities: 2005–2030.

There is no better way to identify the reality of the environment we are attempting to research than by referring to the human element. The following case studies present information about the lives of six individuals with disabilities, with information on services accessed and costs (when available) associated with their needs on an annual basis and projected 25 years out. Four of the cases present information on physical and cognitive disabilities. Given the predictions regarding an aging population, one case is based on a chronic medical condition (diabetes) and another on Alzheimer's. No two case studies were completed in the same state.

Crystal's Story

General Description

Crystal is a one-year-old girl living with her single, 20-year-old mother, Ruth, in Vermont. Crystal was born prematurely at 27 weeks. Crystal and her mother had home health nurse visits because she was at high risk due to prematurity. Crystal's mother and nurse had noticed that Crystal was not developing motor skills normally and had a preference for one side. She was diagnosed with cerebral palsy (CP) at six months. She is now being evaluated for seizures because she has periods of staring.

Crystal is tiny and below normal for weight and height. She is withdrawn and quiet most of the time, although she smiles at Ruth. Crystal's left arm muscles are stiff (spastic) and she does not sit up on her own. She tries to roll over in one direction, although she does not crawl. Crystal coos and makes noises, is bottle-fed, and does well with pureed baby food. She is gaining weight and, like all babies, likes being in her carriage and going for rides.

Crystal and Ruth live in a rented mobile home in rural southern Vermont. The town they live in is 40 minutes from the nearest hospital or city. Ruth worked as a waitress during her pregnancy. She has not returned to work since Crystal was born because of Crystal's medical problems and not having adequate day care. Ruth and Crystal are now on public assistance. Ruth's mother, Jean, lives in the same area and works full time as a secretary for a cement company. She visits Ruth frequently. Crystal's father is not involved with the family.

Diagnosis and Level of Functioning

CP is a developmental disability that appears early in life, manifested by difficult control of movement and posture. With a relationship to the central nervous system and damage to parts of the brain, it may occur before, during, or after delivery. [573] There are four types of CP. Spastic CP, in which the muscles are stiff and permanently contracted, affects 70–80 percent of individuals with CP. Doctors often describe the type of spastic CP an individual has based on which limbs are affected (e.g., both legs, one side, or all four limbs). [574]

It is a challenge to assess Crystal's level of growth and development because of her prematurity, although her type of CP seems to be located on the left side of her body. She can grasp and reach with her right hand and is being evaluated for seizures and mental retardation. About 45 percent of children with CP have epilepsy. Seventy percent of people with CP have other disabilities, including mental retardation. [575] Crystal is too young to be evaluated for ADLs or IADLs.

Present Services and Costs

The home health nurse referred Ruth and Crystal to FIT, the Family, Infant and Toddler Program. FIT is Vermont's response to the Individuals with Disability Education Act (IDEA), which requires states to have a program or services to assess and support children with special health needs and delays in development to reach their full potential. FIT is a family-centered system of early intervention for children from birth to three years who have or may have special health needs and/or delays in development. After age three, the local school system is responsible for the coordination and delivery of supportive and educational services through an Individual Education Plan (IEP).

FIT did the original assessment and referrals for Crystal. Because Ruth has no private insurance, all the costs are assumed by the state of Vermont. If Crystal were eligible for SSI and received Medicaid, some of the cost would be incurred by the Medicaid connection to SSI, which is both federal and state funded. They arranged for Crystal to be seen and followed by a developmental pediatrician who has a monthly Vermont Children with Special Needs clinic in the nearby city. Through FIT, the early childhood educator has developed with Ruth, Jean, and other professionals an IEP for Crystal. Crystal has been assigned a case manager through FIT to help Ruth with access and coordination of services. Crystal has physical therapy twice a week for muscle and joint flexibility and development. She has an occupational therapist who does play therapy and fine motor coordination with Crystal. A dietitian visits with Ruth to talk about nutrition and food planning, because children with CP burn more calories. An early education and parenting specialist works with Ruth, Jean, and Crystal on parenting and bonding with a child with special needs.

A social worker is working with Ruth on her financial and housing situation. The mobile home is not handicap-accessible and the town she lives in does not have a special education department in its school system. They are discussing moving into a more accessible home and considering moving to the city, where more services are available and there is a school with a special education department. If Ruth does not move to the city, Crystal will be transported daily to the city school, which is 40 minutes each way.

The social worker and parenting specialist are concerned about Ruth. She is often overwhelmed with the care of Crystal and her own lack of social contacts. Her friends do not visit her anymore, and she can only go out when Jean can come over and babysit.

Transportation is becoming an issue because Ruth's car is old and she does not have the money to buy a new one. She uses the Red Cross for transportation for medical visits for Crystal. This is a service the Red Cross provides for rural families in southern Vermont.

Ruth is now on public assistance for income through the Office of Economic Services and Vermont Health Access Program (VHAP) for health coverage (Medicaid). She receives a supplemental payment from the state and food stamps. With the help of the social worker, she is looking for funding for a special stroller and chair for Crystal. She may have access to a Payer of Last Resort Pool, which is available through FIT. The state of Vermont has reorganized its agencies for people with disabilities into one department, the Department of Aging and

Independent Living, to better coordinate and administer services to the elderly and individuals with disabilities. (Crystal would be eligible also for an SSI payment and Medicaid through that eligibility, and Ruth would continue to be covered under the public assistance program.)

	Annual Costs
	Public Assistance:
Temporary Assistance to Needy Families	$ 6,420 (2004 dollars) [576]
State Subsidy Payment to Family	$ 2,802 (2002 dollars) [577]
State Flexible Family Funding	$ 1,122 (2004 dollars) [578]
Food Stamps	$ 2,400 (2004 dollars) [579]
Personal health care costs (average personal health costs)	$10,437 (1993 dollars) [580]
Supplemental Security Income	$4,032 (estimated child payment) [581]

Future Services and Costs

In 2030, Crystal will be 27 years old. Crystal's history has been a difficult one. Her mother, Ruth, left her at the age of six. Ruth said she just couldn't take it anymore. They had never moved out of the mobile home and Crystal had been traveling almost two hours back and forth from a special education program in the city. She had no friends locally and was very isolated, just like her mother, Ruth. Jean, Crystal's grandmother, became the parent and guardian for Crystal. They continued to live in rural Vermont and traveled to the school and other services. Jean was better able to cope with Crystal's care, and they developed a very loving relationship. Crystal graduated from high school, but never found employment and had continued to live with her now aging grandmother. They took care of each other. They had refused any services for people with disabilities. They had had no contact with the Department of Aging and Independent Living since Crystal finished high school. When Crystal was 25, Jean could no longer care for herself or Crystal. Jean contacted the Center for Independent Living for help.

Crystal has been assigned a case manager from the Department of Aging and Independent Living. Because she can no longer live with her grandmother, Crystal has agreed to go into a small group home in the city to transition her to more independence and the possibility of employment.

Crystal is able to do all of her ADLs in an adaptive environment. She can walk with a leg brace and cane with some difficulty. She now has a motorized wheelchair. [582] She has the potential to assume her IADLs with adequate training. When she lived with her grandmother, Jean managed the money and shopping.

Crystal had a full evaluation by the Center for Independent Living. She is receiving psychological counseling. Crystal is withdrawn, has low self-esteem, and is moderately depressed. She was rejected by her mother, had no friends due to her rural isolation, and misses her grandmother. She had been evaluated for mental retardation as a child and was found to have normal intelligence. She did finish high school but did not receive any vocational training or further education.

Crystal's plan for independence is full employment, her own apartment, and case management. Crystal agrees with the plan but is not sure she can do it. Her present services through an HCBS waiver include vocational training, psychological counseling, group living, socializing activities at the Center for Independent Living, and IADL training. She visits her grandmother every week. She receives SSI from SSA and medical insurance through VHAP (Medicaid).

Annual Costs

Supplemental Security Income	$ 6,624 (2003 dollars) [583]
VHAP (Medicaid)	$10,437 (1993 dollars) [584]
(average personal health costs)	
Group Housing	$40,000 (2004 dollars) [585]
	(estimated national average)
HCBS Waiver	$35,215 (2003 dollars) [586]

Case Summary

Crystal's story represents a number of themes, including a child with disabilities born in a rural setting, a family caregiver system, the availability and fragmentation of state services, and consumer direction. The rural setting led to financial difficulties and isolation. While the FIT program did provide home visits, for the majority of Crystal's life, the rural setting meant transportation issues, employment issues for the mother, lack of availability of day care and school services, and social isolation from schoolmates and other social services. The state provided intense, family-oriented services and support for the first three years of Crystal's life, but as she grew older, Crystal fell between the cracks and received no services for a period of time. However, at 27, she was able to reconnect to support services provided by the state. The support of her family was mixed. Her mother was overwhelmed and left, and a loving grandmother assumed her care. However, her grandmother continued the social isolation and, therefore, Crystal has been delayed reaching full independence. The level of consumer direction is not clear. Did Crystal prefer social isolation with her grandmother or did she not fully understand her choices? The costs have clearly increased as Crystal has moved from family care to more independent living.

Robert's Story

General Description

A Wisconsin resident, Robert, is a 45-year-old man with schizophrenia complicated by a developmental disability. The voices that he hears constantly and responds to verbally are poorly controlled by medication. He has an average IQ. He is overweight with poor posture, is not secure on his feet, and has a history of numerous broken arms. Although he often looks unkempt, his clothes are clean, his hygiene is good, and he is nonviolent. Robert appears shy and withdrawn when he is fighting the voices and has limited eye contact and slurred speech that he can correct if he is asked to speak more clearly.

Robert was diagnosed with behavioral issues, developmental issues, and emotional disturbance when he was in elementary school. He was placed in a school for emotionally disturbed children, attended public high school with the support of a special needs department, and had some vocational training. When he was 23, he worked for one year in a supermarket but fell and broke his arm. He refused to go back to work.

Robert lives with his elderly, retired parents and goes to day habilitation (sheltered workshop). He had lived in a group home in the past, but he did not want to stay in that setting because he did not like his roommates. For the majority of his life, he has lived with his parents. He is the second oldest of five siblings. Two of his brothers and one sister live nearby in Wisconsin. One sister lives in New Jersey. Robert is very involved with his family and visits his sister in New Jersey every year with his parents. Robert is friendly with some of the participants in his day program. Robert has a network of past teachers and counselors that he calls on the telephone every week. Some of these relationships have existed for more than 30 years. He enjoys music, football, and vacations with his family. He is able to take public transportation and go shopping at the mall by himself.

Diagnosis and Level of Functioning

According to the National Institutes of Health, schizophrenia is a chronic, severe, and disabling condition. People with schizophrenia often suffer terrifying symptoms, such as hearing internal voices not heard by others (hallucinations) or believing that other people are reading their minds, controlling their thoughts, or plotting to harm them. Approximately 1 percent of the population develops schizophrenia—more than 2 million Americans suffer from the illness in a given year. Children over the age of five can develop schizophrenia, but it is very rare before adolescence. Antipsychotic drugs are the best treatment now available, but they do not cure schizophrenia or ensure that there will not be further psychotic episodes. [587]

Robert takes antipsychotic drugs and regularly sees a psychiatrist for medication management. The antipsychotic drugs do not fully control his hallucinations. Over the years, he has been admitted for acute psychiatric hospital care when he is nonfunctioning because of the hallucinations. In a recent hospital admission, he was found to have high cholesterol, for which he now takes medication regularly. After that admission, he was referred to an internal medicine physician for medical care. It is not unusual for people with disabilities to have their medical care focused on their disabilities and not to have recommended preventive examinations and routine screenings.

Robert is able to do his ADLs with oversight from his parents. Robert manages his weekly allowance and is able to go shopping and take the bus. In the past, he has flown alone to visit his sister with his parents getting him on the plane and his sister being there when he arrives. He has not been able to live independently, cook his own meals, or manage a household. Robert participates in decisions about his life and trusts his parents and family.

Present Services and Costs

Robert meets the Wisconsin definition for adults with serious mental illness and, because of his balance and speech difficulties, meets the developmental disabilities definition. Chronic mental illness means a mental illness that is severe in degree and persistent in duration, which causes a substantially diminished level of functioning in the primary aspects of daily living and an inability to cope with the ordinary demands of life, which leads to an inability to maintain a stable adjustment and independent functioning without long-term treatment and support and which may be of lifelong duration. Chronic mental illness includes schizophrenia, as well as a wide spectrum of other severely disabling psychiatric conditions, but it does not include organic mental disorders or a primary diagnosis of mental retardation or of alcohol or drug dependence. [588] An individual who also has been diagnosed with developmental disabilities has more difficulty with daily living skills and often lacks the ability to live without some amount of daily support.

Wisconsin has been a national leader and an incubator in the area of services for the treatment of people with mental illness. [589] The Wisconsin Administrative Code, Chapter HFS 63, mandates each county to have a Community Support Program (CSP).

A CSP is a coordinated care and treatment program providing a range of treatment, rehabilitation, and support services in the community through an identified treatment program and staff, ensuring ongoing therapeutic involvement and individualized treatment for people with severe and persistent mental illness. The array of required treatment services available to CSP consumers includes crisis intervention; symptom assessment, management, and education; medication prescription and monitoring; psychiatric evaluation and treatment; and family, individual, or group psychotherapy. The required array of rehabilitation services available to CSP consumers includes vocational assessment, job development, and vocational supportive counseling; social and recreational skill training; and individualized support, training, and assistance in ADLs. The required array of support services available to the CSP consumers includes assistance in obtaining needed physical and dental care, legal services, transportation services, acquisition of financial support and benefits, and housing supports. Case management is an integral part of CSP services. CSP case management includes coordination of assessment and treatments, coordination of referrals, assessment and monitoring of symptoms, providing supportive therapy, and symptom education. Case management also includes advocacy on behalf of consumers; education, support, and consultation with consumers, parents, families; and other supports. [590] CSP is an HCBS waiver program for Medicaid, and the county in which the program resides pays the state portion. Because the counties are required to know what their constituents want and need, the programs vary by county. There is also a statewide quality assurance program for mental health services to collect client-specific data and measure consumer-oriented quality.

Robert lives at home and attends a day habilitation program that is part of the CSP in the county. Day habilitation provides him with education, supportive therapy, socialization, and other activities. His case manager sees him at least once a month there. He is able take public transportation to and from the program. The CSP also covers his visits with the psychiatrist and medication management.

Robert receives SSI and has Medicaid for health coverage. Robert also receives SSDI and Medicare from his retired parental work record, because he was disabled before he was 22 years of age, was never married, and does not have a sufficient work record of his own.

Robert's parents are both retired and middle class. They are his guardians and have power of attorney. They meet with the case manager once a year and as needed. When they are on vacation and Robert does not go with them, Robert stays with one of his brothers. His parents are members of the National Alliance for the Mentally Ill of Wisconsin and attend the local chapter meetings.

Annual Costs	
Community Support Services	$ 6,030 (2001 dollars) [591]
Community Treatment Services	$ 1,211 (2001 dollars) [592]
HCBS Waiver	$36,528 (2002 dollars) [593]
Supplemental Security Income and Social Security Disability Insurance	$ 7,104 (2003 dollars) [594]
Medicaid plus Medicare (average personal health costs)	$21,236 (2000 dollars) [595]

Future Services and Costs

In 2030, Robert will be 71 years old. As his parents aged, he agreed to live in a community residential home. When his parents were alive, he would come home for a weekend day and his parents would take him out one evening during the week for dinner. After both of his parents died, his siblings assumed the same schedule. He spends one weekend day with one of his three siblings in the area and another sibling takes him out to dinner once a week. His youngest brother is now his guardian and has power of attorney.

Robert still has daily hallucinations. He is more unstable on his feet and uses a walker. He has developed high blood pressure and adult onset diabetes. He is more withdrawn and is often talking back to the voices. He does not want to go to a day habilitation program anymore. He likes to watch television, especially sports, and listen to music. He still spends part of each day phoning friends, siblings, and teachers from his past. He will walk around the yard or sit on the porch. He no longer wants to go on the bus by himself. He can still do his ADLs with reminders from the residential staff; the staff also help him with money management. The CSP provides him with medical care, dental care, psychiatric care, medication management care, and case management.

Annual Costs	
Community Residential Services	$10,159 (2001 dollars) [596]
Community Treatment Services	$ 1,211 (2001 dollars) [597]
HCBS Waiver	$36,528 (2002 dollars) [598]
Supplemental Security Income and Social Security Disability Insurance	$ 7,104 (2003 dollars) [599]
Medicaid/Medicare (estimated average personal health costs)	$21,236 (2004 dollars) [600]

Case Summary

Robert's story represents a number of themes, including the family caregiving system, a well-coordinated state system, and consumer direction. Robert's family has a very strong sense of family responsibility. His parents cared for Robert his whole life while fostering independence and utilizing public and private support. The siblings have continued the support of Robert, as he is an integral member of his family. The state of Wisconsin has well-coordinated services, including acute care and LTC. Robert has benefited from coordinated services and case management. Robert has directed his life with the support of his family. The cost of services has been substantial, even with the family caregiving. The success of Robert's story is consumer direction with active family support in a state with well-coordinated services.

Lucy's Story

General Description

Lucy is an 18-year-old girl with mental retardation. She lives at home in Massachusetts with her parents, who are a lawyer and a manager, and her younger brother, who is four years younger. Their home is in a small middle- to upper-class town northwest of Boston. Lucy attends a public high school. According to Massachusetts Chapter 766 and the Federal IDEA, the public school system must provide her with education and appropriate services until she is 22 years old. Lucy has been attending a full day of classes in the school's special education department. She has had prevocational training to be able to clean trays and tables in the school cafeteria. This year, she will be attending half-day vocational training as a health care assistant and half-day classes in the school's special education department.

Lucy's social activities are parent-directed. She has attended dance classes and theater classes. She is involved and has competed in the Special Olympics for swimming and downhill skiing. She has four girlfriends. Three are from her special education class and the fourth is a girl she has known since elementary school. She usually talks with them on the telephone and attends school activities and dances with them. Lucy has a friend she calls her "boyfriend" whom she met through Special Olympics. She talks with him on the phone, but they do not see each other outside of the Special Olympics. Lucy lives at home with her parents, who have power of attorney for her.

Diagnosis and Level of Functioning

The definition of mental retardation, according to the American Association on Mental Retardation, is as follows:

> Mental retardation is a disability characterized by significant limitations both in intellectual functioning and in adaptive behavior as expressed in conceptual, social and practical adaptive skills. This disability originates before age 18. The five assumptions to the application of the definition are (1) Limitations in present functioning must be considered within the context of community environments typical of the individual's age peers and culture; (2) Valid assessments consider cultural and linguistic diversity as well as differences in communication, sensory, motor and behavioral factors; (3) Within an individual, limitations coexist with strengths; (4) An important purpose of describing limitation is to develop a profile of needed supports; and (5) With appropriate personalized supports over a sustained period, the life function of the person with mental retardation generally will improve. [601]

Lucy has cognitive development delay. Her IQ is 64. Her speech is slow. Her reading, writing, and math skills are at a first-grade level. While she is shy at times, she can be friendly with people she knows, and she communicates back and forth with peers and adults in a limited but effective way. She has no physical limitations or chronic illnesses. She can perform ADLs, such as bathing, dressing, and eating, with reminders from her parents. She would have difficulty with IADLs, such as money management, some shopping, and traveling.

Present Services and Costs

The local education system is responsible for much of Lucy's past training and costs. According to Massachusetts' Chapter 766, the school system must provide education, training, and counseling up to the age of 22. The school has provided a special need education, vocational training, and speech and language therapy to work on her vocabulary, word retrieval, and language processing for appropriate responses. She has had ongoing counseling with the school social worker about adaptation and appropriate social behaviors.

Because Lucy is 18, she is starting to transition to the adult support system through the Massachusetts Department of Mental Retardation. She is presently being reevaluated by the Regional Eligibility Team. The Regional Eligibility Team will do an Individual Support Plan (ISP) to determine the adequate, most appropriate, and least restrictive supports she will need. The ISP will include Lucy and her parents. The local provider for the Massachusetts Department of Mental Retardation, through an approved ISP, will continue her vocational training, provide her with activities for continued socialization, and assign her a service coordinator. The service coordinator is a case manager who will do ongoing assessments and provide information, crisis intervention, and advocacy.

Lucy will continue to live at home while she is in vocational training. She is also staying involved with the Special Olympics. Lucy will no longer be covered by her parents' private health insurance. She will go on MassHealth, which is Massachusetts' Medicaid. She will also be eligible for SSI through the Social Security Administration.

Her family will also be able to access support services. Family support services consist of any community-based service administered or financed by the state MR/DD agency providing vouchers, direct cash payments to families, reimbursement, or direct payments to service providers, which the state agency identified as family support. Examples of family support include cash subsidy payments, respite care, family counseling, architectural adaptation of the home, in-home training, sibling support, education and behavior management services, and the purchase of specialized equipment. [602] While Lucy's family is upper middle class, they take advantage of family counseling and in-home training through the local Department of Mental Retardation provider.

Annual Costs	
Average Cost per Special Education Student	$13,542 (2003 dollars) [603]
Supplemental Security Income	$ 6,624 (2003 dollars) [604]
HCBS Waiver	$42,536 (2002 dollars) [605]
Average MassHealth Cost (estimated average MA personal health care cost, per capita)	$21,820 (2000 dollars) [606]
Family Support	$ 2,653 (2002 dollars) [607]

Future Services and Costs

In 2030, Lucy will be 44 years old. It is expected that at that time she will be working as a health care assistant in an assisted living facility under a supported employment program of the local Department of Mental Health provider and an HCBS waiver. Supported employment consists of MR/DD state agency–financed programs for long-term employment support, with the goal of developing independent work skills leading to competitive wages for individuals with mental retardation. [608] She will be earning minimum wage or above and have her health benefits through her employer.

Lucy will live in a supported living apartment through an HCBS waiver. Supported living includes housing in which individuals choose where and with whom they live, in which ownership is by someone other than the support provider, and in which the individual has a personalized support plan that changes as his or her needs and abilities change. [609] Lucy's housing is provided by the local Department of Mental Retardation. She takes the bus to her job and to go shopping.

Her parents still live nearby and have power of attorney. Lucy, her parents, and the service coordinator are discussing a long-term plan for Lucy as her parents' age. They are discussing whether her brother, who lives out of state, should have power of attorney or whether they should appoint a guardian.

Lucy is still very involved with her parents. Lucy goes to church with her family, goes on vacation with them, and spends holidays with them. She also has social activities through the local Department of Mental Retardation provider. Lucy has a boyfriend whom she sees regularly. Lucy remains healthy, although she is now overweight.

Annual Costs	
Housing Support	$23,752 (2002 dollars) [610]
Employment Support	$12,377 (2002 dollars) [611]
HCBS Waiver	$42,536 (2002 dollars) [612]
Estimated Supplemental Security Income (earned wages would determine exact amount)	$ 6,624 (2003 dollars) [613]
Medicaid	$21,820 (2000 dollars) [614]

Case Summary

Lucy's story represents a number of themes, including the family caregiving system, a well- coordinated service system at the local level, and consumer direction. The success of Lucy's family caregiving is that the family has resources. They are well educated and have a middle- to upper-class income. They know how to advocate for Lucy and foster her independence and socialization. The services available to Lucy are at the local level, including the town school system. The school system coordinates the transition to the local provider for the Department of Mental Retardation. Lucy has the advantage of a local agency that will support and coordinate care and independence. Because her parents have fostered her independence, Lucy can direct her life within the context of her abilities. Many of the earlier costs were assumed by the local school system and her parents. The costs increased as she assumed a more independent but supported life, although she earns an income and has medical coverage through her employer.

Miguel's Story

General Description

Miguel is 27 years old and a resident of Colorado. He sustained a spinal cord injury at the level of T-4 (fourth thoracic vertebrae) in a car accident one year ago. He is wheelchair bound and is in his first year of rehabilitation.

Miguel came to the United States from Central America when he was 12 years old and lived with his parents and two sisters in Arizona. Miguel speaks English and graduated from high school but has poor reading and math skills. Since high school, he has worked in the food industry as a dishwasher and short-order cook. He moved to Colorado three years ago with two friends to work at a ski resort in the kitchen as a cook. The pay was better and the resort offered low-rent housing to the staff. One night, after work, he was in a single-car accident. He hit a patch of ice and went off the road and hit a number of trees. He was thrown from the car and broke his back.

Miguel has had two surgeries on his back. The first was to stabilize the dislocation of his spine with a spinal fusion. Six months later, he had a rod placement to further stabilize his back. He was in rehabilitation after the first surgery. Since the second surgery, he has received his rehabilitation in a nursing home, where he receives both physical therapy and occupational therapy. He is hoping to be discharged to an apartment that is handicap-accessible with the support of a personal assistant.

His parents and sisters from Arizona have visited him three times since his accident and would like Miguel to move back home so they can be more involved in his life. His friends from work visited him at first, but now, a year later, they rarely come by.

Diagnosis and Level of Functioning

Spinal cord injury (SCI) occurs when a traumatic event results in damage to cells within the cord or severs the nerve tracts that relay signals up and down the spinal cord. The most common types of SCI include contusion (bruising of the spinal cord) and compression (pressure on the spinal cord). Severe SCI often causes loss of control over voluntary movement and muscles of the body and loss of sensation and function below the point of injury, including loss of bowel and bladder control and sexual dysfunction. [615]

There are 11,000 new cases of SCI each year, and 247,000 Americans are living with SCI. The most common cause is motor vehicle accidents and the second most common cause is violence, such as a gunshot wound. Most SCIs occur in men between the ages of 16 and 30. Thirty-four percent of SCIs result in incomplete or quadriplegia (paralysis of all four limbs) and 25.1 percent result in complete paraplegia (lower limb paralysis). [616]

Miguel has a spinal cord injury at the T-4 level. He has paraplegia (loss of muscle control and sensation in his legs). He also has some paralysis of his trunk, which means he has difficulty sitting. His injury did not affect his diaphragm and he has no breathing problems.

For his ADLs, Miguel has full use of his arms and hands. He can feed himself and participate in his hygiene and dressing. With rehabilitation and appropriate aids, he will be able to swing his lower trunk and transfer into a wheelchair. With rehabilitation, his ability to balance while sitting and leaning forward, backwards, and sideways is improving. Miguel needs significant assistance in the beginning of the day with hygiene, dressing, and getting in the wheelchair and again with settling for night.

For IADLs, Miguel still needs assistance. The language barrier, especially the written word, is difficult. He does not always understand medical language, consent forms, and instructions. Transportation resources are limited, so his ability to go out of the nursing home is limited. He is able to manage his money.

Miguel is very angry. He is angry about the accident and his injury and has not accepted his disability. His isolation and language issues frustrate him and he feels useless. His psychological state is impeding his rehabilitation and he is receiving counseling from a social worker.

Present Services and Costs

Miguel is presently living in a nursing home that provides rehabilitation, including physical therapy, occupational therapy, and social work. The social worker has helped him get SSI through the Social Security Administration and Medicaid, through the State of Colorado. Miguel now has an income and medical coverage. In the nursing home, Medicaid pays all medical expenses and the SSI is paying for housing and food.

Miguel will have access to services for adults with disabilities through Colorado's Office of Adult, Disability and Rehabilitation Services (ADRS). ADRS's mission is to ensure the safety of Colorado's adults and individuals with disabilities, and their rehabilitation needs. This office promotes personal choice, independence, and improved quality of life. The program goals of this office are to help clients develop and exercise their individual competencies and talents, and to achieve the highest possible levels of rehabilitation, employment, community participation, and independence. [617]

Miguel would like to have his own apartment that is accessible. With a personal assistant in the morning and evening, Miguel could probably live independently. However, in Colorado, there is a waiting list for housing. More than 1,200 families remain on the Supportive Housing and Homeless Programs waiting list for rental assistance. [618] Miguel is on that waiting list.

There is also a shortage of direct care staff, nationally and in Colorado. Miguel cannot go into an apartment without a personal assistant for ADLs. High turnover and low wages have resulted in personal care boarding homes, assisted living, and nursing homes reaching a crisis state for the industry. [619]

The nursing home social worker has also referred Miguel to the vocational rehabilitation program in Colorado, The Division on Vocational Rehabilitation provides job coaching, adjustment training, and on-the-job training to offer one of the best opportunities for individuals with the most significant disabilities to secure and maintain gainful employment in integrated work settings in the community. [620] Eligibility determination is usually completed within 49 days.

Colorado is experiencing the largest shortfall in revenue in over 60 years. Colorado suffered an $869 million dollar shortfall in State FY 2002–03. A $900 million dollar shortfall is anticipated for state FY 2003–04. This will result in deeper and more significant program reductions at the state level. Little assistance from the Federal Government can be expected because recent federal funding is flat. [621] The recovery from Colorado's last major recession, over two decades ago, took 42 months. The recovery from the current recession is projected to be slower and more uncertain. [622] This current fiscal situation in Colorado will result in increasing waiting lists for services and delays in new services, such as expansion of the Independent Living Centers.

Annual Costs	
Nursing Home	$42,000 (1999 dollars) [623]
Health Care and Income	$25,394 (2004 dollars) [624]
Social Security Disability Insurance	$10,404 (2004 dollars) [625]
Estimated Annual Medicaid	$21,457 (2000 dollars) [626]

It is noted that the first year of costs, including health care and living expenses for a person with a spinal cord injury and paraplegia, is $249,549 in 2004 dollars. [627]

Future Services and Costs

In 2030, Miguel is 53 years old and living in a board and care home. Also called an adult care home or group home, this home offers housing and personal care services to between 3 and 16 residents who are assigned to a bed. Group home services such as meals, supervision, and transportation are usually provided. [628] Miguel has a personal assistant for his ADLs when one is available. When one is not available, he pays someone at the board and care home under the table for help. Miguel is capable of assisting with his hygiene and toileting. He can prepare meals, go shopping, and manage his own money. He can transfer from bed to wheelchair and back to bed. He has a motorized wheelchair paid for by Medicaid after he developed chronic shoulder problems from his manual wheelchair. With the motorized wheelchair, he is able to travel where he needs to go in his neighborhood.

Miguel did start vocational rehabilitation but was frustrated by the language barrier and inadequate transportation services. His vocational rehabilitation counselor was concerned about his mental health. They had difficulty finding a Spanish-speaking counselor and Miguel was not open to talking about his disability or his anger. He dropped out of the program because he was frustrated. He has maintained an income through SSDI and SSI and medical insurance through Medicare and Medicaid.

He remains very frustrated by his disability, social isolation, and language barrier. He drinks alcohol daily and is at times belligerent. He has been evicted from other housing situations in the past, and a number of personal assistants refuse to care for him. None of his old friends are in touch with him. His family still calls him and encourages him to come to Arizona, but he is afraid of losing his benefits. His social life is based on the people in his board and care home and the local bars. He has no steady relationships. Because of his drinking, he is on a waiting list for vocational rehabilitation and is not welcomed in an independent living center. Miguel has no case manager or coordination of care.

His health has been affected by his alcohol abuse, mental health issues, chronic urinary tract infections, and pressure sores. The latter two conditions are related to his paraplegia and place him at risk for septicemia, which is an infection of the blood system and can be fatal. He receives his care at an outpatient clinic and the local emergency room. At times he is admitted to the hospital or has home care services for his infections and falls. He does not have a regular doctor and his care is based on each individual incident of infection or fall. He does not have coordinated care, nor does he have any preventive care or screenings. Most of the time, he either does not understand the physician's instructions or he does not follow them. Medicaid covers his occasional prescriptions. He is not receiving any treatment for his alcohol abuse or his mental health issues.

Annual Costs	
Social Security Disability Income	$10,404 (2004 dollars) [629]
Medicare and Medicaid	$16,854 (1995 dollars) [630]
HCBS Waiver (Board and Care Home)	$29,120 (1997 dollars) [631]
Personal Assistance Services (3 hours per day)	$19,656 (2003 dollars) [632]

Case Summary

Miguel's story represents a number of themes, including a language barrier, complications added by substance abuse, lack of a family support system, lack of portability of services from one state to another, and lack of state funding for services. A SCI is a sudden-onset disability, and a negative, angry response is not unusual. An unhealthy response to disability, such as substance abuse, is also not unusual. The entire situation is compounded by the language barrier and social isolation. Miguel is at high risk. Because of a recession and budgetary restraints, state services are not coordinated or even available. There are long waiting lists. His health care is not coordinated. Miguel has and will continue to fall between the cracks. He will not reach his potential for rehabilitation and independence. Without addressing his anger, depression, and alcohol abuse, it is hard to say whether his rehabilitation will ever be consumer directed.

Howard's Story

General Description

Howard is a 72-year-old man living in Redondo Beach, a suburb of Los Angeles, California. Howard lives with his wife, Sophie, who is 68 years old. They have three children, ages 48, 45, and 39, and eight grandchildren. Howard retired five years ago from a small aerospace firm located in Los Angeles, where he worked as a design engineer technician. Sophie also retired five years ago from where she worked part time in a physician's office as a registered nurse. Howard and Sophie live together in a two-bedroom modest condominium three blocks from the Pacific shore. They like to walk every morning along the beach, and twice a week they volunteer at the local high school for literacy program.

Howard and Sophie drive one weekend a month to visit with each one of their children and grandchildren, going to San Diego, Berkeley, and Pasadena. They have a circle of friends their own age who visit together frequently, occasionally meeting for lunch at a local cafe. Howard and Sophie enjoy attending their local community symphony concerts.

Howard and Sophie have been relatively healthy. Howard has some difficulty walking due to a leg injury from an auto accident 25 years ago. However, he is able to walk unassisted. Howard has mild hypertension, which is being treated with an antihypertension medication he takes once per day. Sophie is a breast cancer survivor, and has been disease free for the past eight years. Howard and Sophie have Medicare as their primary insurance.

During the past six months Sophie noticed that Howard was being forgetful, with such things as having read the morning paper, and he increasingly did not recall time spent at the high school literacy program. Recently, Howard was walking with his three-year-old grandson during a visit to San Diego and was unable to remember his way back to his daughter's home one block away. Howard went to his physician and after evaluation was diagnosed with early Alzheimer's disease.

Diagnosis and Level of Functioning

Alzheimer's disease is a disorder of the brain's nerve cells that slowly impairs memory, thinking and behavior, and is eventually fatal. [633] The three stages of Alzheimer's disease follow:

- Mild. A person starts to lose short-term memory. He or she may forget names of friends, appointments, or new information.
- Moderate. The person needs more help with ADLs. Agitation, confusion, and anger are common.
- Severe. The person can no longer make decisions, has difficulty speaking, or may not recognize loved ones. [634]

Disease Impact

- An estimated 4.5 million Americans have Alzheimer's disease. The number of Americans with Alzheimer's has more than doubled since 1980.
- In 2050, the number of individuals with Alzheimer's could range from 11.3 to 16 million.
- Increasing age is the greatest risk factor for Alzheimer's. The disease affects 1 in 10 individuals over 65 and nearly half of those over 85.
- A person with Alzheimer's will live an average of 8 years to as many as 20 years from the time of symptom onset. From the time of diagnosis, people with Alzheimer's survive about half as long as those of similar age without the disease.
- National direct and indirect annual costs of caring for individuals with Alzheimer's disease are estimated at $100 billion.
- Alzheimer's disease costs American business $61 billion a year—$24.6 billion covers Alzheimer's health care and $36.5 billion covers costs related to caregivers of individuals with Alzheimer's, including lost productivity, absenteeism, and worker replacement.
- Seven out of 10 people with Alzheimer's disease live at home, where family and friends provide their care. Additional paid care average $12,500 per year. Families pay almost all of this out of pocket.
- Half of all nursing home residents have Alzheimer's disease.
- The average cost for nursing home care is $24,000 per year but can exceed $70,000 per year depending on the state or area of the United States.
- The average lifetime cost of care for an individual with Alzheimer's is $174,000.
- By 2010, Medicare costs for beneficiaries with Alzheimer's are expected to increase 54.4 percent, from $31.9 billion in 2000 to $49.3 billion.

Medicaid expenditures on residential dementia care will increase 80 percent, from $18.2 billion to $33 billion in 2010. [635]

- On average, a worker who takes care of an older sick relative, such as a person with Alzheimer's disease, loses $659,139 in lost wages, pension benefits, and Social Security income. [636]

Services and Costs

Howard and Sophie attended a local Alzheimer's support group at the recommendation of the nurse practitioner in their physician's office. The support group provided them with information on community resources and a support network of Alzheimer caregivers.

Two years after the diagnosis, Howard was able to remain physically independent. He remained engaged in all his social relationships; however, his memory loss was increasing at a slow but noticeable rate. Howard and Sophie continued to do the activities they enjoyed together. There were increasing times that Howard would become very frustrated and angry at his memory loss. Howard and Sophie discussed Howard's illness with their children and developed a living will outlining Howard's wishes for medical treatment should he become incapable of expressing his wishes.

Three years after the diagnosis, Sophie had to accompany Howard whenever he went outside their home. Howard could no longer drive. He required some help with bathing and dressing, and required the use of a cane when walking. Sophie and Howard visited less with their friends and no longer traveled to see their children. Howard and Sophie stopped their volunteer work. Friends and family were supportive and would visit Sophie and Howard in their home.

Four years after the diagnosis Howard was able to carry on short simple conversations, but his short-term memory was severely impaired. Sophie had to dress and bathe Howard. Howard was incontinent during the night and required toileting reminders during the day. Sophie became dependent upon friends to stay with Howard so she could go the store and the bank and complete errands. Howard had one hospitalization after a fall in the shower. His hospital stay was only two days for evaluation of a possible head injury, at a cost of $3,500. Medicare reimbursement for rehabilitation to the subacute facility was not possible after his hospitalization because Howard did not have a three-day qualifying hospital stay. The hospital case manager arranged for home physical therapy to evaluate Howard and Sophie's home for safety and assistive devices to aid Howard's mobility. Sophie was concerned about being able to manage

Howard alone: getting him out of bed, and in and out of a chair. The Home Health Agency providing the physical therapy did evaluate Howard for home health services and found that while Howard was in need of physical care, his needs were not at a skilled level of nursing care. Therefore, help was not covered under Medicare. The cost of two weeks (6 one-hour visits) of home health services was $2,500. Sophie and her children met together to evaluate the medical resources available to them and to plan for Howard's increasing physical dependence and mental deterioration. The concern of the children at this time was Sophie, who was becoming more isolated and no longer able to provide the total physical care Howard required.

Howard met the eligibility requirements for the California Medicaid Waiver Program. The program is for adults who require nursing facility care but wish to remain at home. [637] Services provided in the home include nursing, case management, therapies, and home aide assistance. A Medicaid waiver allows the state to waive portions of the Social Security Act referring to Medicaid and implement services that otherwise may not be covered under Medicaid, may be more cost-effective, or may enable a senior to remain in the least restrictive environment (i.e., the home). [638] Howard remained in the Medicaid Waiver program for one year at a cost of $14,760. Medicaid Waiver Services provided an aide to bathe Howard and help him into a chair three times per week. A home health nurse visited once per month to evaluate Howard and his care plan. Howard died at home at age 77; Sophie was 73. During Howard's last six months of life, his youngest son, who is single and employed full time, took a six-month unpaid leave from work to stay with Sophie and Howard. The son provided total care for Howard and helped Sophie, who became increasingly exhausted and unable to provide for all of Howard's needs. Howard and Sophie's other two children provided financial support for the son who took a leave from his job.

Case Summary

Alzheimer's disease as depicted in this case is typical of the disease course and impact. Howard's family, namely his wife, was responsible for the majority of his increasing physical needs. [639] Alzheimer's disease, as this case represents, is one that results in caregivers' isolation and causes a long-term burden on a caregiver's emotional, physical, and financial resources. As in this case, the LTC needs of those with Alzheimer's disease are not medically acute or reimbursable under the benefit structure that currently exists.

Elise's Story

General Description

Elise is a 56-year-old African-American woman living in a rural Mississippi community. Elise is a widow, has a high school education, and lives alone. She has two adult daughters; one who lives in New York City and one daughter who is an officer in the Army, currently on active duty and stationed in Germany. Elise works part time (20 hours per week) at a local hardware and feed store as a checkout clerk. Additionally, she works at home babysitting a neighbor's two toddlers three mornings a week. Elise is active in her church and sings in the choir every Sunday morning. Although they are distant in geography, Elise is close to her two daughters. They speak to each other every week by telephone. Elise has several woman friends with whom she socializes on a regular basis. Social activities include church events and a sewing group. Elise does not have a car. She walks to work and church, which are both one block from her apartment.

Elise's annual income from working is $10,400, plus a pension from her deceased husband, which provides her an additional $875 per month. Her total annual income is $20,900. Elise has no health insurance.

Elise has smoked half a pack of cigarettes per day for the past 41 years. She is sedentary in her lifestyle, and is overweight by 65 pounds. Elise was diagnosed with diabetes five years ago and is insulin dependent. She has been hospitalized twice for high blood sugar and has recently had difficulty walking due to an open wound on her left foot. She self-administers insulin. She has a glucose monitor; however, she cannot afford the test strips to measure her blood glucose levels three times per day.

Diagnosis and Level of Functioning

Diabetes is a disease that affects the body's ability to produce and use insulin. Insulin is a hormone made in the pancreas. Insulin is used to get glucose (sugar) from the food eaten into the cells of our body to be used as a source of energy. With diabetes, the body either doesn't make enough insulin or can't use the insulin it produces very well. Glucose then builds up in the blood.

Type 1 Diabetes usually appears in children and young adults, while Type 2 Diabetes usually appears after age 40; however, children who are overweight are at high risk for developing Type 2 Diabetes. Another type of diabetes, Gestational Diabetes, appears during pregnancy. Women who develop gestational diabetes are at greater risk for developing Type 2 Diabetes later in life. In 2000, Mississippi ranked second in the United States in overall prevalence of diabetes, after Puerto Rico.

The Mississippi State Health Department estimates that 9.3 percent of Mississippi's adult population had diabetes in 2001. That's an increase from 7.6 percent in 2000. In 2001, nearly 190,000 individuals age 18 and over reported that they had been diagnosed with diabetes, and estimates are that another 95,000 have not yet been diagnosed. In total, it is estimated that more than a quarter million (285,000) Mississippians had diabetes in 2001. About 750,000 Mississippians are at increased risk of undiagnosed (Type 2) diabetes because of the risk factors of age, obesity, and sedentary lifestyle (lack of exercise). [640]

Diabetes is the seventh cause of death by disease in the United States, affecting an estimated 16 million people nationwide. It is the leading cause of heart disease, kidney disease, adult onset blindness, amputations, and stroke. In Mississippi, according to the Center for Disease Control (CDC), approximately 285,000 people have diabetes. Of those, 90,000 are unaware that they have it. Most people who are undiagnosed have no symptoms.

Diabetes Prevalence

Nationally, 2.3 million (10.8 percent) of African Americans have diabetes; however, one-third of those affected do not know it. In Mississippi, figures for 1996 showed that 56,253 African Americans were diagnosed with diabetes, and a like number of cases went undetected.

- One in four African Americans between the ages of 65 and 74 has diabetes.
- African Americans are 1.7 times more likely to develop diabetes than are white Americans.
- The number of African Americans diagnosed with diabetes tripled between 1963 and 1993.
- One in four African-American women and one out of five African-American men over 50 has diabetes.
- African-American women are at a higher risk for developing gestational diabetes during pregnancy than white women.
- Diabetes is the fifth leading cause of death for African Americans between the ages of 45 and 64, and the third leading cause of death for those 65 and older. [641]

Diabetes Complications

African Americans experience higher rates of at least three of the serious complications of diabetes: blindness, amputation, and end-stage renal disease (kidney failure).

Diabetic retinopathy is a term used for all anomalies of the small blood vessels of the retina caused by diabetes, such as weakening of blood vessel walls or leakage from blood vessels. African Americans are twice as likely to suffer from diabetes-related blindness.

Diabetes is the most frequent cause of nontraumatic lower-limb amputations. The risk of a leg amputation is 15 to 40 times greater for a person with diabetes. Each year 56,000 people lose their foot or leg to diabetes. African Americans are 1.5 to 2.5 times more likely to suffer from lower-limb amputations; 10 to 21 percent of all people with diabetes develop kidney disease. In 1995, 27,900 people initiated treatment for end-stage renal disease (kidney failure) because of diabetes. African Americans with diabetes are 2.6 to 5.6 times more likely to suffer from kidney disease, with more than 4,000 cases of end-stage renal disease each year. [642]

The per capita medical expenditures totaled $13,243 for people with diabetes and $2,560 for people without diabetes in 2002. The projected increase in the numbers of people with diabetes suggests that the annual cost in 2002 dollars could rise to an estimated $156 billion in 2010 and to $192 billion by 2020. [643]

Future Services and Costs

Elise does not qualify for Mississippi Medicaid because her income is greater than $826 per month in 2003 and she has not been determined medically eligible. [644]

In 2005, Elise will have two hospitalizations due to uncontrolled diabetes. The second hospitalization will be for surgery on the infected open wound on her foot. After the surgery, Elise will not be able work her part-time job at the hardware store. She will start the application process for SSI and SSDI.

In 2006, Elise will qualify for Mississippi Medicaid, and receive an annual medical benefit of $2,969. [645] She will also be eligible to apply for both SSI and SSDI through the Social Security Administration, because she is no longer able to work due to her diabetes. This year, Elise had four more episodes of acute uncontrolled diabetes. She has not been able to return to her part-time job. She is at high risk of a below-the-knee amputation caused by the early stages of necrosis in her lower left leg. The medical expenses for Elise in 2006 are $20,500.

Late in 2006, Elise will have a below-the-knee amputation and experience a postoperative heart attack. She will be admitted to a nursing home posthospitalization and will undergo a slow recovery and rehabilitation. The expense of the surgery and nursing home care will be $38,000.

By the end of 2006, Elise will no longer be able to participate in her social activities or maintain her home without assistance. She will become depressed and withdrawn, and will not follow her prescribed diet, exercise, or insulin regime.

Elise is admitted to a nursing home after a lengthy hospitalization and development of a larger right leg ulcer, which is failing to heal. Elise spends the next two years in a nursing home ($16,010 per year) under a Medicaid benefit. [646] If she had SSDI, Medicare would also provide medical support to the nursing home. In addition to the nursing home stay, Elise has four acute hospital admissions. She undergoes a right below-knee amputation and experiences a second heart attack due to severe vascular disease caused by the uncontrolled diabetes and smoking history. Elise continues to live in the nursing home. In 2009, she signs advanced directives defining her wishes for no further treatment to prolong her life.

Elise has six hospitalizations in 2009 at a cost of $72,000. Each subsequent hospitalization is due to vascular insufficiency, heart failure, and renal failure caused by uncontrolled diabetes. Elise refuses dialysis for the acute renal failure. She expires in January 2010 in the nursing home. The cause of death is acute renal failure. The total medical expenses for Elise's care from 2005 to 2010 was more than $202,000.

Case Summary

Diabetes is a disease characterized by a lack of control of blood sugar. Although inadequate control of blood sugar levels can cause acute clinical problems and require hospitalization, in general, the most common health consequences of diabetes are chronic rather than acute. [647] Elise's case exemplifies the chronic characteristics of diabetes: poor healing of a lower leg wound leading to amputation, compromised cardiac function, and an increasingly impaired renal function. Her disease was difficult to control because of her excess weight, smoking, and inability to monitor her blood sugar. Progression of disease eventually affected Elise's ADLs and IADLs, making her totally dependent on others for her care.

Case Studies Summary

These six case studies move the discussion from the abstraction of numbers and dollars to real people and their families in a struggle to find a coordinated, comprehensive response to their LTSS needs. Despite the diversity of challenges associated with varying types of disability and multiple secondary conditions, the underlying human element is the desire to live independently and with dignity.

The examples of real-life struggles today and projected changes 25 years later in 2030 help capture both the complexity and significance of designing an LTSS system sooner rather than later. Several key findings can be offered from an analysis of the six life stories of individuals with chronic, intellectual, physical, and mental disabilities.

The current system of responses to individual needs is dependent on state-specific differences in coverage and resource allocation. Families and friends are a critical component of an informal caregiving system that is eroding as America ages. Without federal intervention and financial assistance, no state can begin to cope with the growing demand for HCBS. Current state and federal budget deficits and funding priorities jeopardize a patchwork system of services and supports that do not meet the current needs of the target population, let alone those projected into the future.

Summary of Findings

LTSS cannot be looked at in isolation from other health care needs, including acute care and mental health service needs. The range of needs across age and type of disability highlight the importance of service coordination, access to information, and need for support of the family as well as the individual with disabilities. Current costs are not a customized response to individual needs. Costs reflect matching an individual's circumstances to available services and supports, based on federal eligibility criteria, with degrees of consumer choice and direction varied based on the state in which the individual lives. Medicaid, Medicare, and Social Security dominate the cost profiles and projections, with the quality of services and support most evident with active family intervention. The projected costs are dependent on, at a minimum, no loss of entitlements as we know them today. The evolution of a consumer-responsive comprehensive system demands additional analysis of the costs of raising and supporting, at home and in the community, individuals across a spectrum of functional need from birth through the aging process. Supporting families in their unpaid caregiving will help keep public costs lower. However, the balancing of public and private responsibility for caregiving must be confronted directly by policymakers through incentives, respite options, flexibility, and portability of services and skills training.

Part VII

MOVING TOWARD REFORM

Defining Who Needs LTSS

The development of public policy for LTSS requires finding a common ground for defining eligibility. There is not yet a common agreement among the critical stakeholders as to who needs LTSS. Most data and definitions are based on individuals age 65 and older. The definitions range for the target population from a medical diagnostic approach to a functional assessment. It is impossible for policymakers and researchers to accurately calculate current and future costs without a clear consensus as to who should be covered by an LTSS system.

Growth in Population Over Age 65 Needing LTSS

Regardless of the definition of the target population, there is clear and undisputable data that the number of people over age 65 with ADLs and IADLs is growing and will double by 2030. Twenty percent of people age 65 and over will require assistance with at least one ADL, and 50 percent will require such assistance by age 85. People in need of assistance with two ADLs will grow from 1.8 million to 3.8 million by 2045.

Declining Disability Prevalence for Individuals Age 65 and Older and Rising Disability Rates for Those 65 and under

The research concludes that disability has declined in the 65-and-older population using ADLs and IADLs as measurement. It is less clear whether this decline is due to health improvements or environmental changes aided by increased use of durable medical equipment, including assistive technology. The prevalence of disability in those 65 and younger is rising using the chronic condition definition of disability. The increased longevity of people with lifelong disabilities and its impact on the need and future costs for LTSS are unclear from the current literature.

Changes in Disability Prevalence Across the Age Span and Their Impact on Future LTSS Costs are Unclear

There are 38 million people under age 65 reporting some level of disability; of this group, 25 million have a specific chronic disability. Depending on the definition used, the estimated population in need of LTSS under age 65 ranges from a conservative figure of 3.5 million to more than 10 million.

As the prevalence of disability and use of LTSS increases in the under-age-65 population, it is unclear from the research what effect this growth will have on the future costs and services of the LTSS system. It is less clear how many individuals under the age of 65 are in need of assistance with ADLs and IADLs when different definitions of disability are used. There is no aggregated data on the overall costs of LTSS using the NCD/AARP definition, which includes transportation, nutrition, and housing. It is less clear what services and supports truly look like for individuals under age 65, across disabilities and specific age groups, for those working and living independently. The research shows that individuals under age 65 are heterogeneous and have specific needs according to gender, age, and type of disability.

Disparities in LTSS Needs Among Minority Populations and Impact on Future LTSS Costs

A further challenge was found in understanding the correlation between the disparities in LTSS needs among minority populations and the impact on future utilization and costs for LTSS. Black children were reported to be 13 percent more likely than white children to have a reported activity limitation. A recent GAO study confirmed that the black population has higher disability rates and lower lifetime earnings and shorter life expectancies than whites. The issues of poverty, lack of insurance, and continued segregation from affordable and consistent health care will increase the future needs and costs for LTSS for a population that is projected to make up 50 percent of the American population by 2050.

Individuals with two or more ADL limitations and personal assistance needs under the age of 65 estimated a shortfall of 16.6 hours of help and were more likely to be nonwhite females and to live alone. People who live alone are 10 times more likely to go hungry, 20 times more likely to miss a meal, and 5 times as likely to lose weight. Paid assistance for personal assistance services (PAS) goes primarily to people 65 and older, and working-age people 65 and under rely more on unpaid PAS.

Growing Prevalence of Mental Illness and Impact on Future LTSS Costs

The prevalence of chronic disease and deaths caused by noncommunicable disease in the United States will increase from 28.1 million to 49.7 million between 1990 and 2020, an increase of 77 percent. Mental illness will rank number two after heart disease and will replace cancer by 2010 as having a greater impact on death and disability. Medicaid is the principal public payer for mental health services and represents (36%) of the $48 billion in spending. It is unclear what the future LTSS needs and costs will be for this population.

Uncertainty of Future Utilization and Costs for LTSS

Future utilization and costs for LTSS are highly uncertain because of the rising cost of health care, fiscal challenges of federal and state governments, increased longevity of high-cost disability populations, increased prevalence of chronic conditions, and the changing philosophy regarding where and how LTSS are delivered.

There are 57 million working-age Americans (18–64) with chronic conditions such as diabetes, asthma, and depression; more than one in five (12.3 million) live in families that have a problem paying medical bills. The number of chronically ill people with private insurance who spend more than 5 percent of their income on out-of-pocket health care costs increased from 28 percent in 2000 to 42 percent in 2003, a 50 percent increase to 2.2 million people. Less than 55 percent of people with chronic conditions receive scientifically indicated care, and the "defect rate" in the quality of American health care is approximately 45 percent.

The impacts on LTSS costs for 6.6 million individuals with chronic care needs who are uninsured and go without needed care (42%), delay care (65%), or fail to get needed prescriptions (71%) are unclear, but without timely intervention they will affect future need and costs.

Eligibility and service pathways to state Medicaid programs have expanded to meet the growing needs of their uninsured and LTSS beneficiaries and reflect the growing challenges of economic downturns, increased health premiums, increased longevity, a low savings rate, and slower wage growth. The ability of states to respond to current and future LTSS needs is beyond their capacity and resources.

Medicaid Has Added Many New Eligibility Pathways and Programs Over Its 40-Year History and Extends Benefits to Many Middle-Income Americans Who Are Aging and Faced With Catastrophic LTSS Costs

Two-thirds of Medicaid spending is for population groups and services technically defined as optional; these services account for 90 percent of all LTC Medicaid services. Optional services are currently undergoing cuts across the country as states struggle with unsustainable growth in costs and caseloads. It is unclear how vulnerable people with disabilities are, with the majority of their services and funding falling into optional categories.

Seventy-five percent of HCBS waivers are for people with MR/DD and are used to purchase LTSS. The other 25 percent are used for people with physical disabilities and older people. Three small waiver programs serve individuals with a primary diagnosis of mental illness, accounting for 0.2 percent of HCBS waiver expenditures. Further research is needed to explore the LTSS needs of the other 25 percent using HCBS.

Medicaid spending for acute care and LTC for the blind/disabled category was $91,889 billion; $51,733 billion for the aged category; and $59,022 billion for children, adults, and foster care children.

All Medicaid beneficiaries, when broken into the following three categories, demonstrate a high vulnerability to rising health care costs and dependence on family members for health coverage and LTSS:

Almost 70 percent of the Medicaid caseload (18.8 million) are children; the rest are adults who rely solely on Medicaid for both Medicaid and SCHIP for an entire year.

About 12.3 million used both Medicaid and SCHIP for part of the year and were uninsured for two-thirds of the months they spent without Medicaid/SCHIP; job-based health insurance covered nearly all the remaining months over an entire year.

About 9.7 million never relied solely on Medicaid during the year and had other sources of coverage; less than 23 percent were children, but nearly half (46%) were seniors.

Most Uninsured Americans Are Working and Many Are LTSS Paraprofessionals

Forty-nine percent of uninsured Americans are either self-employed or work for companies with fewer than 25 employees or fewer than 10 employees, of which only 52 percent offer insurance. Over 50 percent of low-income employees of small firms with incomes below 200 percent of the federal poverty level are uninsured. Over 2 million health care paraprofessionals do not work full time, do not receive benefits, and report wages below the poverty line.

Private LTSS insurance is targeted to individuals age 65 and older and highly targeted to specific diseases such as Alzheimer's. More than 6 million Americans own LTSS insurance, and 50 percent of the claims paid are for Alzheimer's and other forms of dementia.

The risk of disability during a worker's career is significant, as are the consequences to the individual's and the family's financial security. The risk of disability is higher than premature death and is higher for older people than younger people; females are more likely to become disabled than males. A 45-year-old earning $50,000 per year and suffering a permanent disability could lose $1,000,000 in future earnings. The public underestimates the help that is available from public disability insurance programs (SSDI and other state-mandated, short-term programs). Workers compensation benefits cover only disabilities caused by injury or illness arising on the job—only an estimated 4 percent of disabilities.

Lack of Data on Current and Future Costs for the under- and over-65 Populations with Disabilities Raises New Questions for Researchers and Policymakers

The documented growing demand for LTSS in the home and community raises new questions for researchers and policymakers about current costs and projected future costs for the under- and over-65 populations with disabilities. The cost conundrum is exacerbated by four important factors.

First, there is insufficient data on LTSS costs for individuals under age 65 across the spectrum of disabilities. Second, there is insufficient data on the costs of responding to a decreasing population of informal caregivers and the development of an approximately trained and paid workforce. Third, there is a lack of agreement on the role and responsibility of the government versus individuals and families to cover the costs of current and future LTSS needs. Without research to explore different public and private cost-sharing scenarios that focus on the under-age-65 population with disabilities, it would be difficult to explore the relationship of public financing and private insurance.

Disability Insurance Is the Missing Piece in the Financial Security Puzzle for Americans with Disabilities

The forth and final factor transcends the specific challenges of development of a responsive LTSS system for the targeted population. The global economic picture and changing demographics, in addition to the current federal budget deficit, raise questions about the political will to maintain current entitlements, let alone craft a new system.

The Issues of Identification of Current and Projected Future Costs for LTSS Are Further Complicated by the Role of Formal and Informal Caregiving, and by Workforce Shortage and Retention Issues

There are 44.4 million American caregivers age 18 and over who provide unpaid care to an adult age 18 or older. Six out of 10 of these caregivers work while providing care; most are women age 50 years or older. The value of donated care is estimated to be more than $200 billion, and it is unclear from the literature how the changing demographics will affect the unpaid care industry and whether there will be cost-shifting to paid care as fewer women become available in the future.

It is unclear who is going to meet the growing demand for providing services and supports as the role of the informal caregiver decreases. The workforce shortage is both a supply and demand problem. As the 65-and-over population increases, the 65-and-under working-age population will decrease and there will be a shortage of workers and taxpayers. In addition, there is a shortage of nurses and home care workers for LTSS. Jobs for nurse's aides are expected to grow by 23.8 percent, while the employment of personal care and home health aides may grow as much as 58.1 percent between 1998 and 2008. It is unclear how many workers (the "gray market") are hired and supervised by consumers who pay for their own care, although the numbers are thought to be substantial.

Direct care workers (3.1 million) are in short supply and have nearly a 100 percent turnover rate in nursing facilities; home care agencies have annual turnover rates of 40–60 percent. Direct care workers have low median hourly wages of $9.20 an hour, and one-fifth (far more than the national average of 12–13 percent) earn incomes below the poverty level; 30–35 percent of all nursing home and home health aides who are single parents receive food stamps. The financial ability for this sector to generate higher wage and benefits is limited by the constraints of third-party payers, such as Medicaid or Medicare, which are and will continue to be pressured to reduce costs under the weight of a growing retirement and disability population.

Americans with Disabilities Struggle to Find a Coordinated, Comprehensive Response to Their LTSS Needs Despite the Diversity of Challenges Associated with the Varying Types of Disability

The current system of response to individual needs is dependent on state-specific differences in coverage and resource allocation. Families and friends are a critical component of an informal caregiving system that is eroding as America ages. Without federal intervention and financial assistance, no state can begin to cope with the growing demand for home and community based-services. Current state and federal budget deficits and funding priorities jeopardize a patchwork system of services and supports that do not meet the current needs of the target population, let alone those projected into the future.

LTSS cannot be looked at in isolation from other health care needs, including acute care and mental health service needs. The range of needs across age and type of disability highlights the importance of service coordination and access to information, and need for support of the family as well as the individual with disabilities. Current costs are not a customized response to individual needs. Costs reflect matching an individual's circumstances to available services and supports, based on federal eligibility criteria, with degrees of consumer choice and direction varying according to the state in which the individual lives. Medicaid, Medicare, and Social Security dominate the cost profiles and projections, with the quality of services and support most evident with active family intervention. The projected costs are dependent on, at a minimum, no loss of entitlements as we know them today.

The evolution of a comprehensive, consumer-responsive system demands additional analysis of the costs of raising and supporting, at home and in the community, individuals across a spectrum of functional need from birth through the aging process. Supporting families in their unpaid caregiving will help keep public costs lower. However, the balancing of public and private responsibility for caregiving must be confronted directly by policymakers through incentives, respite options, and skills training.

Americans with Disabilities Need to be Represented in the Current Public Policy Discussion about the Future of LTSS

How Americans will decide to solve the current demographic challenges of an aging and growing disability population is unclear. Few proposals have provided a total picture of what LTSS means to people with disabilities from birth till death.

As Americans age there will be fewer workers contributing to the pay-as-you-go resources in Medicare and Social Security to keep even the current system afloat. It is unclear how Americans with lifelong disabilities under age 65 can become self-sufficient and economically independent through work and build careers without substantial LTSS reform that allows asset growth and public support for LTSS. It is unclear how Americans will provide for their own health care and services and supports in the future without substantial savings and insurance against the risk of disability.

LTSS Are Not Portable Across States

LTSS are not portable and cannot be moved with an individual from state to state, and current LTSS costs are not a customized response to individual needs. Current costs reflect matching an individual's circumstances to available services and supports, based on federal eligibility criteria, with degrees of consumer choice and direction that vary according to the state in which the individual lives. The fiscal health of each state and its ability to provide the necessary match to draw on federal Medicaid resources determines the scope and array of LTSS for seniors and low-income Americans with disabilities. The personal assistance service needs of an individual in California could be similar to those of someone living in Mississippi and yet the availability of services and funding would vary dramatically.

INDEX

D

E

G

F

H

I

N

Q

R

U

T